THE DANTEUM

A STUDY IN THE
ARCHITECTURE OF LITERATURE

THOMAS L. SCHUMACHER

PRINCETON ARCHITECTURAL PRESS

Published by
PRINCETON ARCHITECTURAL PRESS
40 Witherspoon Street
Princeton, NJ 08540

©1985 by Thomas Schumacher
and Princeton Architectural Press.
All rights reserved.
90 89 88 87 86 5 4 3 2
ISBN 0-910413-09-6
Printed in the United States of America.

Book and jacket design by Eric R. Kuhne.
Giorgio Cuicci's introduction was translated
from the Italian by Michela Nonis.
Scattered quotes reprinted from *Paradiso*
(copyright 1975) with the
permission of Princeton University Press.

For
Marcia
Jerry
Colin
Julius

Dante Alighieri, Death Mask.

CONTENTS

Preface   *1*

Introduction by Giorgio Ciucci   *4*

The Danteum Project   13

Terragni and His Sources   41

The Danteum Design   75

The *Relazione*   *95*

Terragni and Dante   135

Documents   *155*

Index   *164*

PREFACE

Writing about an unbuilt work is difficult. For Terragni's Danteum the problem is further compounded because, unlike Le Corbusier's Maison Dom-ino, Michelangelo's facade for San Lorenzo, or Wright's Mile High Skyscraper, this particular project is little known. Why the Danteum? Terragni's Casa del Fascio and the Casa Giuliani-Frigerio are more interesting projects, more complete, probably more important, and certainly easier to document. The Danteum would not even be known to us had not Terragni's partner, Pietro Lingeri, wanted the project close to him and carried it to his home in Tremezzo just before American bombs destroyed his studio in 1944. The project was not published until 1957, and the lovely watercolor panels were first published in color in 1976.

My reason for choosing to document the Danteum is twofold. First, the Danteum is a modern building concerned with history, a "connotative" building by an "abstract" architect. Second, it required traditional, "natural" materials *and* an advanced system of construction.

I became interested in the Danteum when I read the excerpt from the *Relazione sul Danteum (Report on the Danteum)* published by Bruno Zevi in *Omàggio a Terragni,* his anthology of Terragni's work; [1] I wondered why more of it had not been included. Enrico Mantero excluded the final report from his collection of Terragni's writings, although he included many other unpublished drafts. When I obtained a copy of the manuscript, I was further perplexed by the lack of knowledge about this building. Here was an architect telling us exactly what he was trying to do without resorting to humanistic platitudes, even if he did fall into some ungainly rhetoric; in this way, in form and content the report resembled those of students I had heard in juries. I realized that there was more to the Danteum than had been suspected.

The *Relazione* led me to Milan, to the office of Lingeri's sons, Angelo and Piercarlo, who sent me to their mother, Editta Lingeri, in Bolvedro di Tremezzo on Lake Como. The memories of the hospitable Lingeri family gave me much of the historical background of the project.

Architect Emilio Terragni provided me with patient assistance in deciphering many of his uncle's uncatalogued sketches and numerous photographs. Architect Luigi Zuccoli helped me with his acute memories of Terragni and the project.

There are many to whom I owe thanks for support and criticism. To Aldo Norsa, Gabriele Milelli, and Luciano Patetta, for their ideas and suggestions and their help in gathering information; to Princeton University, for the sabbatical semester that enabled me to begin the project; to the American Philosophical Society, for a grant that enabled me to finish the project; to Giorgio Ciucci, my editor for the first (Italian) edition, whose criticism and patience were constant; to Judy de Maio, for an important perception that led me into an entire new area of search; to Kathy Kenfield, whose editing of the English text for the first edition helped me to clarify many critical issues; to Judy McClain-Twombly, who clarified the text further for this edition; to Kevin Lippert and Eric Kuhne, whose ideas on production made the text so much better; to Teresa Fiore, for an elegant translation into Italian; to Wayne Storey, for his perceptions on Dante; and special thanks to Peter Carl, whose profound and incisive criticisms at the outset of my research gave me the inspiration to delve into the project in a way that I had not previously imagined.

T. L. S.
Charlottesville, Virginia

2

1. Bruno Zevi, *Omàggio a Terragni* (Milano: Etas-Kompass, 1968).

3

INTRODUCTION

Thomas Schumacher's close and thorough analysis of Terragni's Danteum is an invitation to look at this architect's oeuvre in a more complex and detailed fashion, and to observe through it the relationship between literature and architecture. Manfredo Tafuri, in his essay "Terragni's Masques," published in *Oppositions* 11, had already focused his attention on the abstract nature of Terragni's thought, abstracted both from the reality that surrounded him and in the way he formulated his poetics. Tafuri concluded by pointing out the "lost," i.e., "out of place," element in all of Terragni's work, which was, according to him, a sign that the architect was being uprooted from his physical context.

Taking into account both Tafuri's remark and Schumacher's accurate text — which was written long before Tafuri's essay appeared in *Oppositions,* we may begin to set forth a few thoughts and considerations, which complement both works and can be considered an introduction to the analysis of the Danteum.

The Casa del Fascio elicited a strong reaction not only among the traditionalist and monumentalist academic circles, but also in the "rationalist" element of Italian culture. For example, Giuseppe Pagano, in *Casabella* 110, vehemently condemned the building, labeling it pretentious, and furthermore accused Terragni of being an eccentric narcissist.

We can understand the criticism from both fronts a little better if we consider that Terragni's point of view on architecture contained both abstract formal elements and references to the ideal, which could make reference to the history of the city without being "eclectically antihistorical," and thus avoid its participation in "history in the making." Marcello Piacentini's project for the city of Brescia, in which he tried to reconstruct the ancient forum, and Pagano's interest in a residential and fully serviced city are at opposite ends of the spectrum: for the former, the purpose is to express and render immediately perceptible the ancient Roman element of fascism; for the latter, on the other hand, to invest the city with the desecrating images of the fascist revolution.

Terragni's work lies close to the metaphysical experiences of earlier years, and especially to the historicizing elements in metaphysical painting. He also owes something to the Milanese "neoclassicist group," and especially to Giovanni Muzio, its foremost architect. One has to go beyond the "Gruppo 7" declarations — such as the one which expresses " ... sincere admiration for all the architects who have immediately preceded us ... and gratitude for their having been the first to break away from a tradition of superficiality and bad taste ... [we] are trying to follow in their footsteps ... " — to notice that what really stands out in the work of these Milanese neoclassicists is the use of abstract formal elements, receding axes of symmetry, invisible connection lines, and vague indications of perspective depths. In Muzio's Ca' Bruta these elements are spread like fragments on the wall surface, and become "signs" that organize the design and simultaneously do not take away from the fragment's identity (*figures 1 and 2*). In both Muzio's and Terragni's work we find the idea of the city built with fragments, which relate to one another according to a neoclassical order in Muzio's case, and a classical order in Terragni's case. Their work focuses on the recomposition of absolute form, even though their results are very different. The rules and elements that they adopt are atemporal fragments of a whole that doesn't exist anymore, and are explicitly related to a language that can only be rescued by using a different grammar. Following similar hypotheses, though with different shapes, Muzio and Terragni do not negate the city as it exists, but rather embrace historical shapes and meanings. Muzio rereads Palladio, keeping in mind eighteenth-century Milanese neoclassicism; Terragni, in the Casa del Fascio, focuses on the Italian tradition of the "palazzo nobile."

They both seem to be aware of the conflict between the physical reality of the historical relationship, which is established among buildings of different styles, and eclecticism, which is essentially antihistorical. As Tafuri points out, each arrives at a metaphysical dimension in which objects and buildings have no place and, in fact, no longer need one. Accordingly, the Danteum, which is thought out and designed in strict formal and dimensional relationship with its preexisting physical context, starts to assume — because its structure so closely resembles that of the *Divine Comedy* — a metaphysical dimension that goes beyond the physical environment. Once we enter the Danteum and find ourselves within the internal logic that governs the shapes and spaces, we are immersed in the Dantesque condition: Hell, Purgatory, and Paradise are not clearly defined spaces, they are non-places.

1, 2 Giovanni Muzio, Ca' Bruta, Milan, 1919–1923.

As Schumacher points out, the spiral around which the Danteum is organized leads — in Terragni's mind — to infinity, to the absence of place. Theoretically, the building has no need to relate to or to exist in a physical context. The absence of a "place" for the fragments floating on the facade of the Ca' Bruta is similar to the urban uncertainty of the Danteum: the latter is built on the basis of the dimensions of the Basilica of Maxentius, and transcends them through the logic of its internal structure; the former refers to Milanese neoclassicism, and transcends it because of the way the fragments relate to each other. Both aspects relate to the Casa del Fascio: an object that creates a void around itself.

The physical place in which these fragments exist — the wall surface of the Ca' Bruta, the historical site of the Danteum, and the urban void for the Casa del Fascio — is a limited space on which we must write a text: we cannot go beyond the limits of the space, yet this restriction must not interfere with the meaning of the text. Furthermore, it is the text that chooses the context: whether it's the paper on which to print, the marble on which to engrave, or even the margin of another text on which to annotate.

Once again we must go back to the relationship between Terragni and Bontempelli, on which both Tafuri and Schumacher, as well as many others before them, have insisted. Bontempelli wrote, in his magazine *900*:

> Our only instrument of work will be imagination. It is necessary to relearn the art of building, to invent entirely new myths capable of begetting the new atmosphere that we need in order to breathe. We will be done with amusing ourselves by grotesquely gathering up in a butterfly net our weakest sighs, with continually dancing in a circle, stirring up around our bodies the phosphorescent mist of our most closely held impressions. We will be finished when we have placed before us a solid new world. Then our most alert work will be climbing and exploring it, to hew heavy blocks of stone and put them one on top of the other to erect solid buildings, changing ceaselessly the crust of the reconquered earth. [1926]

Ezio Bonfanti wrote perceptively about the affinities between Bontempelli's "magic realism" and the "magic" interpretation — inspired by the metaphysical climate — that Muzio gave to the Ca' Bruta. These attitudes represented a way to dominate everyday life and its contradictions, to repropose them instead as exceptional values; a way to nullify the physical attraction of a language without wounding the creative imagination, which in turn made it possible to transmit meaning beyond judgments like "beautiful" or "ugly," with which most work is greeted often.

We find ourselves in between neoclassicism, in the sense of a return to order, and classicism, intended as the language inherent to the new order that fascism wants to represent. Terragni's rationalism is a "true" classicism, based on purity, the absolute, proportion, mathematics, and the "Greek spirit." There is no need to invent an ideological content, but only to transmit meanings. Terragni's architecture presupposes a given order, in which purity already exists.

The Danteum is an elaboration of absolute form. It is the search for an abstract formal logic, which is based on the structure of the *Divine Comedy*. It reveals a content that, on the one hand, reflects and updates Dante's experience (Schumacher points out the many affinities between Dante and Terragni) and his political message, useful to Italian Fascism, and on the other is also a celebration of Dante. Its meaning is not just what we find in the *Divine Comedy* or in other works by Dante — it is implicit in the very act of building the Danteum, a space in which to celebrate "the greatest of Italian poets." The structure of Dante's text is the abstract element that one can use to build an abstract formal logic. According to Terragni,

> The Architectural monument and literary work can adhere to a singular scheme without losing, in this union, any of each work's essential qualities only if both possess a structure and a harmonic rule that can allow them to confront each other, so that they may then be read in a geometric or mathematical relation of parallelism or subordination. In our case the architecture could adhere to the literary work only through an examination of the admirable structure of the Divine Poem, itself faithful to a criterion of distribution and interpretation through certain symbolic numbers: 1, 3, 7, 10 and their combinations, which happily can be synthesized into *one* and *three* (unity and trinity). [From *Relazione sul Danteum,* published in this

volume.]

The way the first is constructed becomes the structure of the other's text. But structure is not yet architecture. In 1931 Terragni wrote:

From lintel to arch, from cross-vault to dome, Geometry and Mathematics have offered architecture the means to build temples, basilicas, bridges, aqueducts, and cathedrals from the tracings of a plan. But no geometric formula, no law of physics, could have determined the harmony of the masses or the play of the volumes in the light. The elements of construction are the basis, i.e., the alphabet, with which an architect can design in a more or less harmonious fashion. Architecture is not simply construction, or even the satisfaction of material needs; it must be something more. It is the force which disciplines these constructive and utilitarian properties in order to achieve a much higher aesthetic value. Architecture will superimpose construction only when the beholder will be forced to stop and observe, excited and touched by the harmony of proportions in front of him.

Terragni's projects find their place in between this separation of structure and harmony, of construction and architecture. There is really no difference between the abstract and universal language of geometry and mathematics that Terragni speaks of and objectification of language through translation that Bontempelli attempts. The geometrical shapes and numbers are the schema, the plan, but they cannot transmit harmony; and language, on its own, cannot communicate myths. For Terragni, the necessity to communicate harmony and myths — through an abstract imagery which goes beyond an everyday life in which we recognize numbers and language, to that magic realism that reproduces a kind of "atmosphere being born" — becomes a part of "life, even the most everyday and banal, seen as a kind of miraculous adventure, as a perpetual risk, and as a continuous exercise in slyness and heroism. The very act of making art becomes a continuous risk" *[900]*. The risk of incommunicability. Carrà's *Metaphysical Muse* has no face; objects and fragments speak for her (*figure 3*). Sironi's *Traveler* wanders, anonymous and lost, in an urban periphery with which he cannot communicate (*figure 4*). And the objects that Terragni has designed wander, like silent travelers, in an everyday reality from which they have been

10

3 Carlo Carrà, *The Metaphysical Muse*, 1917. The objects speak for her.

4 Mario Sironi, *The Traveler*, 1924. He wanders in an urban periphery, where he no longer communicates.

uprooted and with which they are in conflict. The object is itself abstract, unreal, and metaphysical. However, the possibility of creating and communicating myths is born from this conflict between everyday reality and magical objects.

In the Danteum the equilibrium of numerical rhythms and harmonic relationships is arrived at through the discipline of classicism. This discipline, in its rigidity, in its immobile perfection, in its silent essence, conflicts with everyday life, with the inertia of the masses, and shakes them up. This is the challenge that transforms the banality of everyday life into adventure, and construction into architecture. In 1933 Le Corbusier, in the conclusion of his speech at CIAM IV in Athens, had exclaimed, "My dear comrades and fellow Congress members, let us run toward adventure, the great adventure! Architecture and Urbanism!"

The spaces that Terragni designs are voids, which do not need the beholder in order to exist. His buildings possess, as pure objects, a "classic" equilibrium, which clashes against the meaning of their image in everyday life, an image that the buildings carry in themselves, because they are also "construction." The abstraction is complete, and the myth that the buildings are trying to transmit — in this particular case the unity between Church and Empire that fascism brings about (according to Terragni) and which Dante tries to build in the *Divine Comedy* — exists because it is an artifice that has become reality. The Danteum is the reconstruction of a space in which to live a miraculous adventure. The adventure is that "higher aesthetic value," and can be reached only through formal and logical relationships that one can build following an abstract and nearly invisible trace.

The encounter between metaphysical objects appears to be interrupted and suspended in this building outside time. Our astonishment ceases. We have gone from the physical reality of an historical dimension to the metaphysical dimension of a space without context. The harmony that "will force the beholder to stop and observe, excited and touched" — the architecture capable of communicating myths — happens only in the absence of place, utopia.

Giorgio Ciucci

In a complete and successful work there are hidden masses of implications, a veritable world which reveals itself to those whom it may concern — which means: to those who deserve it.
Le Corbusier, A New World of Space

Fascism, and Mussolini himself, could neither carry out a cultural revolution nor wholeheartedly accept the interpretations of academic culture. Hence a growing indecision and uncertainty of aim.... To the mature regime, all philosophies were acceptable, providing they acknowledged the supreme genius of the Duce.
Adrian Lyttleton, The Seizure of Power

THE DANTEVM PROJECT

THE AVANT-GARDE IN ITALY IS NOT SO EASILY DIStinguished from the rear-garde of Germany or U.S.S.R. during the same period. From the initiation of the movement toward an International Style, Italian architects oscillated between embracing orthodox modern positions and maintaining old certainties. "'The new architecture, the real architecture, must derive from a strict adherence to logic, to rationality,' said the 'rationalist manifesto.' They added, 'For us, in particular, there exists a certain substratum of classicism ... a spirit of tradition.... '" [1] While similar ambiguities may be seen in Le Corbusier's writings of the same period, the seeds of a return to national characteristics can be said to have been sown by the first *rationalists*. [2]

Part of this ambivalence may be ascribed to the fact that the modern movement in Italy was imported *after* Mussolini had seized power, so that the avant-garde found itself having to adjust to an ever-changing and conservative social order masquerading as revolution. Giulio Carlo Argan explains this predicament for Terragni and indeed the whole modern movement:

> The extraneousness of the "foolish" revolutionary ambitions of
> culture to the fascist revolution, the revolution as an unknown
> which one cannot account for, and which avoids fixed values

and denies a political capacity to cultural advances: this was the struggle of artists who had looked to give life to a second avant-garde after futurism.... When Terragni began his artistic career the ideological question was already out of the way. [3]

Beyond the fact that, until the Ethiopian war, the entire world (including Italian architects) considered Mussolini the savior of Italy and a great international statesman, it would have been political suicide for architects to have usurped the role of politics in creating well-being. The Corbusian position that "the happy towns are those that have an architecture.... It is a question of *building* that is at the root of the social unrest of today," from *Towards a New Architecture,* simply would not wash. For the fascist hierarchy, the happy towns were those that had a *torre Littorio,* and many an architect of the day had at least one to his credit. The *torre Littorio,* or Lictor's tower, was one of the traditional symbolic elements adapted from Italian culture without formal alteration from its original use as the urban *campanile.* [4] It was clear that display superseded social or political content. And if the architecture of the period registers anything of its contemporary political condition, it is just that lack of social commitment.

The social pretensions of the International Style were among the first manifestations that the Italian avant-garde discarded during the early thirties, when the polemic turned toward nationalism (*figure 5*). With the celebration of the first decade of fascism in 1932, the beginning of heightened nationalism surrounding the Ethiopian war, and the Great Depression, the avant-garde all but abandoned those arguments that had drawn architects into CIAM in 1928.

Those factors alone did not change the polemic. Part of the shift in architectural ideology came in response to the argumentative brilliance of Marcello Piacentini, the leader of the Roman school now known as the "monumentalists" (*figure 6*). Piacentini was the "evil one" of Italian modern architecture. After Speer, he was the most powerful architect of the period. As director of *Architettura* he controlled much of what Italians read concerning their own architecture and foreign work.[5] Piacentini mounted a critical attack on modern architecture that modernists could not refute, because it was oriented to their own viewpoint: function, structure, and the conditions of the modern industrial world. He "exposed the emperor" by displaying peeling plaster,

14

underused spaces, leaking roofs, overheated rooms, etc., and implied, in a rational and eminently reasonable way, that modern architecture possessed a symbolic basis, not a technical one. [6]

Piacentini's writings during the early thirties show little trace of his allegedly narrow view of the elements of architecture. His denial of the need to fit all buildings with the "arches and columns" proposed by Ugo Ojetti [7] as essential to an *Italian* architecture makes Piacentini sound modern in rhetoric, though he rarely used modern architectural forms. [8] Repostulating the notion that all building activity need not necessarily result in *architecture,* [9] he proposed to divide the built environment into two types: one clothed in "underwear" and the other in "evening dress." [10] The overt pluralism of this attitude showed genuine political acumen. It was perfect for the mentality of Mussolini, who thrived on his ability to turn real losses into apparent gains and who trod a fine line between inaction and defeat.

Meanwhile the rationalists had turned to the nationalistic drive of the *state* and directed their polemic toward a single aim: to persuade Mussolini that modern architecture could symbolize the fascist revolution, its system and hierarchy. They did not succeed; however, this signified neither the neutralization of modern architecture in Italy nor the success of the forces of reaction. Mussolini never made the decision for or against modern design. Unlike Hitler or Stalin, he felt equally at home with modern or classically derived forms (depending on the context of "theater" he would be involved with at the moment) as long as the grandeur of the regime was expressed. The rationalists demonstrated without doubt that modern architecture could muster a monumentalism comparable to Roman revival.

Much of the architecture for the state realized in the *stile Littorio* (that crude collage of Roman, neoclassical, and modern that is often identified with any fascist regime) came late in the thirties, after Mussolini had begun to align himself with Hitler. Modern design, in fact, was still alive and well when the war ended the fascist era, and a surprising continuity exists between building forms of the late thirties and late forties, despite the fact that many of the most talented and productive personalities, including Pagano and Terragni, died during the war.

The characteristic arches and columns of the Piacentiniani — with an occasional "*fascio littorio* order" — can be contrasted to the equally rhetorical use by rationalists of the concrete frame. (The creation of rhetorical columns out of the *fascio littorio,* symbol of *fascism,* is not far removed from Latrobe's adaptation of the corn husk and tobacco plant as orders for the new American Republic.) The frame's frequent appearance elicits speculation that it was intended as the symbolic equivalent of the orders (both based on a construction technique at their origins). In the polemics the avant-garde made a strenuous effort, especially after the Ethiopian war, to disassociate itself from the International Style and *esprit nouveau* symbolism, which might be mistaken for liberal, even Bolshevik, leanings.

The rationalists' problem was to maintain as much "modernity" (in terms of a grammar of architectural forms) as possible without adopting a machine aesthetic that would have appeared to devour national characteristics. Terragni's Casa del Fascio in Como, then the most famous building in Italy, imbues the resulting, most often *abstract,* aesthetic (*figure 7*). [11] In the writings of the period, Pagano best summarized the aesthetic "retreat" in *Casabella:* "We cannot any more consider the aspiration of Le Corbusier to an absolute technology as the 'style' of our epoch daily fixed [by that technology] ... the position that we must assume today is a rigorous aesthetic one." [12]

While Pagano's 1933 statement foreshadowed the pragmatism of Italy's economic isolation later in the decade, the resulting economic policy — the *Autarchia* (self-sufficiency) — had little effect on design practice. One of the most important effects of the Autarchia was the reduction of imported iron ore for steel production; but modern buildings used little more steel than traditional buildings, despite the polemics of modern architects. The psychological shift was more important, however, swinging some architects toward the more famous Italian natural materials like travertine, marble, and tufa. The rationalists had already absorbed traditional joinery and construction techniques without losing the abstract qualities of the International Style. Terragni's major buildings, for example, were faced in tiles or marble, not stucco.

An abstraction that avoided either extreme — International Style and monumentality — was not without symbolic intention. On the

16

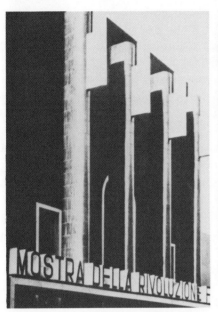

5 Adalberto Libera and Mario de Renzi, Tenth anniversary exhibit of the Fascist Revolution, Palazzo delle Esposizioni, 1932. "Art Deco" fascio littorio columns in the service of the State.

7 Terragni, Casa del Fascio, Como, 1932–1936. View from the Via Pessina. A modern palazzo, the "Marble House of Fascism."

6 Marcello Piacentini, Monument to the fallen of WWI, Bolzano, 1931. A fascio littorio order, like Latrobe's corn husk and tobacco orders for the infant U.S.A.

contrary, Terragni explained the design of his Casa del Fascio according to its place in the symbolism of the regime, stating, "Here is the Mussolinian concept that Fascism is a glass house into which everyone can peer, giving rise to the architectural interpretation that is the complement of this idea: no encumbrance, no barrier, no obstacle between the political hierarchy and the people." [13] He followed Piacentini's directive for a building in "evening dress," but substituted a sheer *crepe de Chine* for the requisite brocade.

In other words, the rationalists designed as they pleased, more or less, working around political circumstances with the tenacity of the *seicento* painters confronted with the inquisitions of the counterreformation. Even in Rome, rationalists like Adalberto Libera and Mario Ridolfi continued to design buildings that resembled those of northern European modernism well into the war period, and many rationalist works were still being published by Piacentini at that time.

The Danteum, a patently modern building, was enthusiastically received by Mussolini in late 1938 and might well have been built had not the war occurred. The *Relazione sul Danteum (Report on the Danteum),* written to accompany the drawings, resembles Terragni's Casa del Fascio report, complete with the nationalistic ramblings that would certainly have pleased the Duce.

Even a cursory reading of the *Relazione* establishes Terragni's intention to create a *symbol* (Terragni calls it a temple) that would transcend the politics of fascism and respond to a more general, more important, more universal standard of Christian philosophy, a philosophy grounded in his devout (if personal) Catholicism. [14]

Abstraction, symbolism, nationalism, internationalism: the polemic of the middle and late thirties had begun to resemble a Pirandello play, with reality masked by pronouncements and by the ambiguity of architectural forms read as political symbols. Terragni's buildings throughout the period reflect such ambiguity. He created an abstract architecture *and* an architecture of connotation in the facades of the Casa del Fascio in Como, calling the building the *glass house of fascism.* His abstraction was *Italian,* displaying the abstract surface characteristics of that style. His symbolism was *Italian,* making political metaphors, and *Internationalist,* residing beneath the surface qualities of imitated detail, within the realm of *parti.*

IN 1938 RINO VALDAMERI (1889–1943), A MIlanese lawyer and the Director of the Royal Brera Academy in Milan, proposed to the Italian government that a Danteum be created in Rome to celebrate the "greatest of Italian poets," and be built for the planned Exposition of 1942 (called E'42; the Exposition was canceled because of WWII). [15] The Danteum was to be an organization as well as a building, and Valdameri proposed a statute to bring it into being.

Valdameri was a great lover of Dante and was president of his own Dante society, the *Società Dantesca Italiana,* with its center in Milan (the society occupied the same address as his law office). Because he was a fascist (he became a party member in September 1922 and participated in the March on Rome), his interest in Dante related directly to the imperial ideals of Fascist Italy. Among his political-literary activities was to commission an expensive edition of the *Divine Comedy* with illustrations by Amos Nattini, two volumes of which were completed and presented to Mussolini. [16] To realize his dream of a "Danteum" in Rome, Valdameri enlisted the aid of a Milanese steel industrialist, Count Alessandro Poss, who offered the sum of two million lire as a personal contribution for the erection of the Danteum. At the time of this offer, October 1938, the drawings for the Danteum were under way already, and the architects, Giuseppe Terragni and Pietro Lingeri, and the clients were summoned to the Palazzo Venezia for an audience with Mussolini (Thursday, 10 November 1938, 5:30 p.m.) to present the project. [17] The project was apparently well received, and the architects then went on to build a model of the building. [18]

Lingeri's long friendship with Valdameri dated back to his education at the Brera; he and Terragni had designed projects for Valdameri prior to the Danteum commission. Lingeri alone designed the three artists' studios on the Isola Comacina on Lake Como and the seaside villa for the lawyer in Portofino (not executed). Terragni and Lingeri, with Figini and Pollini, prepared drawings for an academic building on the grounds of the Brera Academy, which also was not executed.

The purpose of the Danteum as an *ente* (an official organization) and a building was specifically outlined in the statute that Valdameri drafted to bring it into being. The statute began:

1. A "Danteum" is to be created in Rome: A National

Organization that proposes to erect, on the Via dell'Impero, in this epoch, in which the will and genius of the Duce have realized the Imperial dream of Dante, a Temple to the greatest of Italian poets.

2. The Danteum is proposed to:

a) carry out the celebration of the words of Dante, considered a primary source for Mussolini's creations;

b) aid in its continuous dissemination;

c) construct a library complete with all that is needed for students of Dante; to keep in its collection all the illustrations totally or partially inspired by the *Commedia* and the *Vita Nuova,* and all that is of interest to the iconography of the poet;

d) promote in Italy and foreign lands courses on Dante, to become the living center of any studies and research related to the works of the poet;

e) to suggest and aid those initiatives that foster and attest to the character of Imperial Fascist Italy. [19]

Intended as a symbol of Dante's political aspiration for Italy, the Danteum was to resemble any number of nationalistic monuments, glorifying the arts before politics, but ultimately tying together the two.

The fascists snatched up Dante's political aspiration for Italy and read his works purely for such allegory. Like Saint Francis, whom the fascists used as a symbol of abstinence for an underdeveloped Italy in the midst of the Great Depression, Dante became the harbinger of, and justification for, Italian expansionist policies. The plastic arts used culture heroes as well, particularly in architecture, whose history, especially by the late thirties, was being written to justify Italian imperialism. [20]

Valdameri was careful and politic in choosing the directorate for the Danteum organization. Because Terragni and Lingeri were polemical modernists and the Danteum building was to rise on a sensitive site, it was necessary to gain the support of every minister and officially endorsed intellectual possible. [21] Valdameri proposed a directorate of twenty members to serve without pay "under the watchful eye of the Head of State." [22] Among the various ministers and their representatives would be the president of the *Società Nazionale Dante Alighieri,* the "official" Dante society of Italy founded in 1902. The president of the *Società Dantesca Italiana* (Valdameri) would also sit on the board.

In addition, several personages were chosen for their obvious influence, which would get the project built. Alessandro Poss, the financial sponsor, and Giovanni Gentile, the great intellectual and student of Benedetto Croce, and the most important fascist philosopher, were among them. Perhaps the most significant name on the list was Ugo Ojetti, an influential writer and industrialist, whose polemics against modern architecture were vitriolic and well known. [23] To place Ojetti on the board of directors would most certainly eliminate his possible criticism of the building design, criticism that would have been published in the influential northern Italian newspaper, *La Stampa*.

The project seems to have run into problems after the initial presentation. Between 10 November 1938 and 19 April 1939 there is no extant official correspondence, leading to the speculation that the sponsors and architects were working on the design. On 19 April 1939 Valdameri heard from the special secretary to the Duce, Osvaldo Sebastiani, asking him to request an audience with Mussolini in which the head of state might indicate some directive for the development of the project. Upon receiving this note at the Albergo Ambasciatori in Rome, Valdameri wrote to Mussolini a sycophantic letter in which he promised to devote his energy and his youth to the works of the regime, indicating a desire to provide aid in "various ways" to the Corporazione della Siderurgia (Steel Manufacturing Corporation). The audience never took place. Back in Milan, Valdameri wrote again to Mussolini, indicating that he and Poss had "faithfully executed your orders" (significantly undocumented; was it graft?), and that if the Danteum were to be ready for E'42, it would be necessary to subject Mussolini to another review of the project. He then requested another audience, which took place on 8 May 1939 with Poss.

At this time Mussolini was moving to ally himself with Hitler; it was in May 1939 that the Pact of Steel was signed. Obviously his energies were focused on European politics and not cultural affairs. Valdameri tried unsuccessfully to obtain another audience on 5 June. On 11 August he wrote to Sebastiani to request another date; Sebastiani responded on 4 September (three days after Hitler invaded Poland). He said, in effect, that the time was not ripe and that in "more favorable days" the matter could be brought up again. [24]

Sebastiani's short note concludes the extant correspondence, and by that time the project was effectively a dead letter. Valdameri did not live to see the end of the war. He died 10 June 1943, one month before Terragni.

The correspondence suggests the character of patronage under fascism: a constant "bowing and scraping," offerings of presents, aid, and contributions to the regime.

While the manifest function of the Danteum was to serve as a museum and library, housing all the available editions of Dante's works (as well as works on Dante), the major spaces of this large building were designed to represent the *canticas* of the *Divine Comedy,* intended as a symbol of what Dante represented in politics — Italian unification and imperial pretensions. The appropriateness of choosing a site in the Via dell'Impero (*figure 8*) then, was well recognized by Terragni as " ... confirmation of Dante's 'dowry' of prophecy." [25]

For Terragni, Dante represented both the ancient and the medieval; Mussolini, however, was a rabid Romanist, and the Middle Ages was not a healthy period for the Roman Empire. [26] Despite this seeming conflict, Dante's imperial prophecy was strong enough, when coupled with his vivid imagery of the Empire's future, for Mussolini to place him in the category of Empire Poet.

Thus the architect chose the relationship of medieval to ancient as a primary inspirational motif, and incorporated it into the Danteum site and building program. Because it was neither simply a government building nor a monument to Italian war dead (a typical fascist program), the Danteum project possessed a dimension for the Italians that went beyond political symbolism.

The architects prepared an elaborate set of watercolor drawings on rigid panels at a scale of 1:100. Mario Sironi, commissioned to provide bas-relief sculptures for the facades, made charcoal sketches, which were photographed and montaged onto the drawings (*plates 6 and 7*). These originals were lost in the 1944 bombing of Lingeri's studio.

Terragni drafted the *Relazione,* which was probably not presented to Mussolini in the November 1938 audience. Early in 1939 the poet and litteratus Massimo Bontempelli wrote to Lingeri stating that he received a copy of the report, and that he had sent the drawings on to Marino Lazzari, the director of the National Fine Arts Commission; [27] nothing

8 Via dell'Impero (Street of the Empire), today
Via dei Fori Imperiali (Street of the Imperial
Fora). The Danteum site is to the right, the
Victor Emmanuel monument in the background.

seems to have come of this effort. Besides this, Bontempelli's relationship to the project is unclear. He was most likely a source for Terragni about the relationship between literature and architecture. Terragni and Lingeri were anxious to get the project going, and would have appreciated help from their close friend. [28]

What remains of the *Relazione sul Danteum* is a rough, typewritten draft, composed for illustrations to be inserted into the text. Although large portions are missing, the report is complete enough to piece together Terragni's architectural intentions. The drawings and model were saved from destruction when Lingeri brought them to his villa on Lake Como. The project was one of Lingeri's favorites, but he was responsible in part only for the design development, not the initial concept; while the authorship of a given design bearing both architects' names may never be determined, Terragni clearly *conceived* the Danteum. [29] He worked on the project in Como and in Milan at Lingeri's studio, where he virtually lived with the Lingeri family. [30] Some of Terragni's preliminary drawings, including rough sketches and some mechanically drawn preliminary plans, and the *Relazione* draft are from his studio in Como. The panels and the model remain in almost perfect condition.

Missing from the *Relazione* are the supposed illustrations, the first page of text, and an undetermined number of final pages. Judging from the fact that Terragni scrawled the word "Danteum" across page two, the remaining pages were lost before the war. The panels are rendered in a hard-line ink style overlaid with a lyrical watercolor wash on watercolor paper. The model, recently restored, is rendered completely white, like the intended marble of the building.

THE DANTEUM SITE, AT THE INTERSECTION OF Via dell'Impero ("Street of the Empire," now Via dei Fori Imperiali or "Street of the Imperial Fora") and the Via Cavour (*figure 9*), was intended originally for the National Fascist Party headquarters (Palazzo Littorio), a competition that Terragni and Lingeri had entered as a team in 1934 and placed among the finalists. Directly across the Via Cavour is the Torre dei Conti, a medieval tower and emblem of the Middle Ages, Dante's epoch. Across the Via dell'Impero stands the Basilica of Maxentius, important symbol of ancient Rome. Between the two monuments lies the site for the Danteum, an irregular quadrilateral into which is inserted the rectangular building (*plates 1 and 2*). The description in the *Relazione* explains the sequence and composition of the building (parts of which I will quote at length).

The entire building generates from two figures: a golden-section rectangle (the long side of which equals the short side of the Basilica of Maxentius) and two overlapping squares (*figures 10 and 11*). The golden-section rectangle is Terragni's tie to the ancients, as "one of the plan forms frequently adopted by the ancient Assyrians, Egyptians, Greeks, and Romans." [31] It was also his insurance that the " ... value of 'absolute' geometric beauty [be imprinted] onto the entire structure of the monument." [32] Overlaid on this "theme of the rectangle" is a pair of squares, overlapping in plan and deriving from a variety of sources in Terragni's work and in other architects' buildings. [33] The purpose of this overlap is multiple, but its practical function is to create entry to the building. Terragni explains the square as:

> the most easily perceived characteristic of the work ... revealed in the plan of level 1.60m and in the approach to the study rooms on the ground floor (*figure 12*). The same scheme is created on the opposite side [of the building] where the frontal wall is displaced in front of, and parallel to, the major side of the golden rectangle, thereby creating another pure square. [34]

The system of the original compositional figures is then followed in sequence by a series of smaller-scaled figures, in which

> the mathematical and geometric correspondences can be traced in turn for the most important divisions of the rooms of the building — deriving the workings of the plan from the decompositions of the golden rectangle (*figure 13*). [35]

The sequence of spaces is Terragni's conflation of concepts found in the *Divine Comedy* (the creating of a setting for the poem) and an interpretation of Mussolini's New Roman Empire. [36] The first element we encounter is a freestanding wall (*plate 3*), a facade

> disposed parallel to the front and [displaying] a long frieze of relief sculptures ... that hides the building, creating an internal street of slight incline that leads to the entry and leaves the view to the Colosseum visually free for the visitor who approaches from Piazza Venezia (*plate 4*). [37]

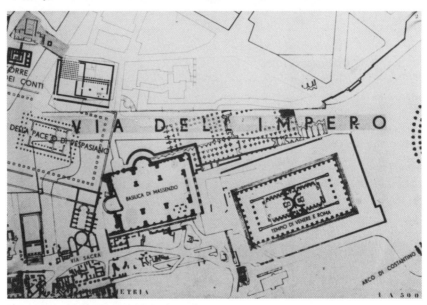

9 Danteum. Small site plan of the immediate area. The Colosseum is to the extreme right.

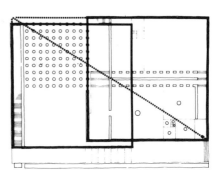

11 Danteum. System of generating squares and the initial golden section created by pulling apart the squares.

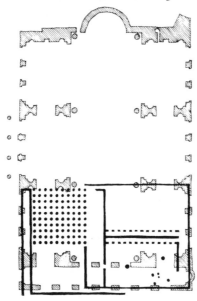

10 Plan of the Danteum superimposed onto the plan of the Basilica of Maxentius.

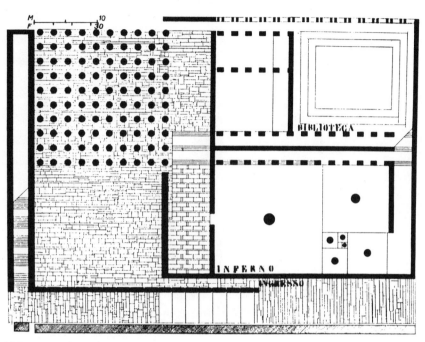

12 Danteum. Plan at 1.6 meters above the street, ground floor.

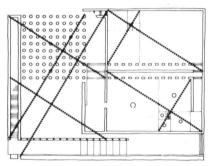

13 Danteum. The decomposition of the golden sections. All major walls and columns fall on one of these lines.

In addition to its pragmatic function the wall was to become

> an immense blackboard, a monumental tablet filled with 100 marble blocks (equivalent to the cantos of the *Divine Comedy),* each in a size proportional to its place in the scheme of its canto.... The tercets or the verses containing the allusions, the references, and the allegory to the Empire will be incised on the facade within the blocks corresponding to the canto from which each is derived. [38]

Passing behind this facade, and through the overlap zone of the generating squares, is an act that Terragni likens to a similar act in the *Divine Comedy:*

> The entrance to the building (*figure 14*), then, situated parallel to and behind the facade, and between two high walls of marble, further restated by another long wall parallel to the front, can also correspond to ... a Dantesque "justification": "I do not know how I entered" (canto I, 10). This securely establishes the character of pilgrimage that visitors must make, lining processionally in single file, and guided only by the intense sunlight that will be reflected on the square space of the court.[39]

The courtyard that follows this narrow passage forms one quarter of the rest of the composition (*plate 8*). "To the functional plan scheme of a cruciform shape that determines the partitioning into *one* (open court) and *three* (the large temple-like rooms dedicated to the three *cantiche*) ... is overlaid a scheme of vertical measure.... " [40] The three spaces dedicated to the *Comedy* are placed in ascending order and occupy the remainder of the rectangle. The courtyard itself is "excluded from the scheme of the *three* fundamental spaces"; [41] while *not* a part of the *Divine Comedy,* the courtyard is elaborately justified by Terragni. The court is "intentionally wasted from the point of view of building economy, and we can thus speak of a reference to the life of Dante up to his thirty-fifth year of age, a life of transgression into error and sin, and therefore 'lost' in the moral and philosophical balance...." [42]

Traversing this court the visitor finds himself in a "forest" of 100 columns, similar to the forest Dante entered in Canto I of the Inferno (*plate 9*). "Each [column] supports an element of the floor above.... This architectonic motif, of great plastic effect, is first of all the

entry portico to the rooms of the Danteum." [43] From this space, or
from the rear of the building, the visitor would be able to enter the
study center, labeled *biblioteca* on the plans (and rather small compared
to the rest of the building). He may instead pass through a corridor
and up a few steps to the first of the only two literal "doorways" in the
building (the other is at the end of the sequence). The route takes him
past five freestanding (presumably) marble figures (*figure 15*), which are
missing from the drawings but included in the model. [44] The figures
represent the damned in agony and are a prelude to what lies beyond
this "gate of Hell."

The atmosphere of the Inferno, like that of the entire Danteum, was
to suggest Dante's pilgrimage (*plates 11 and 12*):

> The spiritual reference and direct dependence upon the first
> canto of the Poem must be expressed in unmistakable signs by
> an atmosphere that influences the visitor and appears physically
> to weigh upon his mortal person, so that he is moved to ex-
> perience the "trip" as Dante did. [45]

The danger of falling into "rhetoricism," as Terragni termed it, was
obvious. It was necessary, then, "to reexamine the problem with our
minds liberated from the preoccupation of literally following the text of
the Magnificent Account." A more abstract setting was necessary; one
that " ... through the balanced proportion of its walls, ramps, stairs,
ceilings, the play of its ever-changing light from the sun above, can
give ... the sensation of contemplative isolation, of removal from the
external world.... " [46] The resulting room dedicated to the Inferno is
thus a simple rectangle divided according to

> a rigorous application of the harmonic rule contained in the
> golden-section rectangle; this results in a series of squares,
> which are disposed in a descending spiral, and which are theore-
> tically infinite in number. In order to stop this decomposition
> at a practical number of squares, we set a limit at seven. Ente-
> ring the room one passes from the first square of seventeen me-
> ters on a side to the seventh of seventy centimeters on a side.
> The continuous line that passes through the center of these
> squares is a spiral, the spiral that results from the topography of
> the *Divine Comedy,* Dante's trip across the abyss of the Inferno
> and the mountain of Purgatory. [47]

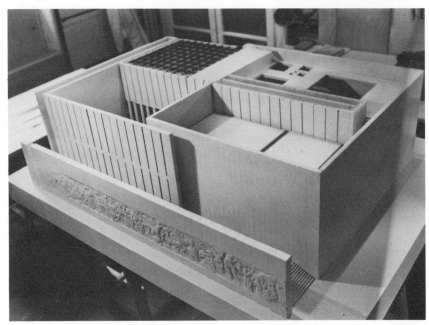

14 Danteum. Model view. The serpentine route begins at the entrance.

15 Danteum. Model. The damned writhing in agony: "They tell, and hear, and then are hurled below." The portal behind is the only doorway in the entire building.

The room self-consciously imitated the architecture of "the Orient, Greece, Italy, Egyptian rooms, Hellenic temples, Etruscan tombs." [48] Terragni perfected this impression in the manner of a stage set, although he was quick to deny a cheap theatrical character for his building:

> The sensation of the *impending*, of the void formed under the crust of the earth and through a fearsome seismic disorder ..., can be plastically created by the overall covering of the room.... [The] fractured ceiling and the floor, which is decomposed into diminishing squares ... will give the catastrophic sensation of pain.... The seven columns, then, have thicknesses proportional to the weight they support.... The imaginary line that collects the group of columns in a spiral assures that such an arrangement ... will produce a sure plastic effect. [49]

The transition from the Inferno to the Purgatory is made by slipping out of the corner of the first space and climbing a long stepped ramp to enter the second space by "insinuation" (*figure 16*). The room itself is equal to the Inferno in size and shape, but the atmosphere is decidedly different. Terragni's reliance on Dante's structure manifests itself in abstracted versions of Dante's own realms, e.g., "the form of a truncated conical mountain ... an island in a sea of water ...," [50] with a contrast "between the void of the infernal chasm and the solid of the mystical mountain of Purgatory." [51]

The room of the second *cantica* "presents analogies with the preceding room. The subdivision of the golden rectangle into seven squares is identical but reversed in direction.... The outline of the fascias is clearly shown ... which is nothing more than the proposition of the 'frame' of the hypothetical structure, in terraces, of the mountain of Purgatory" (*plate 13*). [52] In what is perhaps an unintended theatrical metaphor, Terragni explains the intent of the second room:

> The scene that we intend to prepare to properly present this second *cantica* does not omit such a poetic sensation. And by making use of the abundant light from the wide rays of sun that burst through the ample openings in the ceiling, we will succeed in creating an ambience in which the visitor feels a salutary sensation of comfort, calling his attention to the sky again, but

framed by geometry.... [53]

This is also the place where Terragni's surviving text trails off. But even the incomplete text makes his intentions clear: to create a " ... plastic fact of absolute values spiritually chained to Dantesque compositional criteria." [54] The intent is carried through in the Paradise and in the special room dedicated to the Empire and its reincarnation.

To ascend to the space that represents Paradise the visitor must exit Purgatory at the corner and climb a stairway of three groups of three steps, placed in the zone of overlap of the two squares of the original generating scheme (*figure 17*). The stairway is narrower than the previous transition (it is the same width as the entrance to the building), perhaps symbolizing the soul's difficult ascent to Paradise. This space underwent the greatest decomposition of the three, since materiality is least important here. But Terragni created this effect through the destruction of material and architectural form rather than through the absence of such form (*plate 14*). The visitor enters an antespace, similar to the ante-Paradise of the *Divine Comedy*. He may then go on to the space of Paradise proper or to the space of the Impero. From the antespace the structure of the Paradise is evident: thirty-three columns of glass support a transparent frame open to the sky, surrounded by walls that are further decomposed along the same grid, with glazing between the blocks supported by the columns below; the entire space floats (*plate 15*).

The design displays the golden-rectangle scheme along with the scheme of the superimposition of the square. In the Paradise the golden-section rectangle includes the antespace and the adjacent space at the top of the stair that leads back down to the street. The square removed from the rectangle describes the Paradise proper and corresponds to the limits of the column grid and the transparent beams that frame the view to the heavens.

The progression from dense to framed to open — Inferno, Purgatory, Paradise — following a scheme of ascent to the most holy and sacred space leads the visitor finally to the room dedicated to the New Roman Empire (*plate 16*). This long corridor-room displaces space from both the Inferno and the Purgatory and lies parallel to the axis of the Via dell'Impero, restating the connection of the Piazza Venezia and the Colosseum, thus making the Danteum a microcosm of Terragni's

32

conception of the Empire.

The interdependency of the Paradise and Impero (and their literal separation) symbolizes the interdependency of the Church and the Empire, each of which Dante believed derived its powers directly from God. Terragni makes clear his hope for this state of affairs:

> This room of fundamental spiritual importance comes to represent the germ of the architectural whole.... It therefore can be interpreted as the central nave of a temple, dominating and giving light to the minor spaces. The reference to the theme is clear: The universal Roman Empire that was envisaged and forecast by Dante as the ultimate purpose and the only remedy for saving humanity and the Church from disorder and corruption.[55]

The final descent is made by slipping through the two walls at the far end of the Paradise (the second portal) (*figure 18*) and descending the stair to the street, completing a circuit begun at the entrance of the Inferno. Upon his descent the visitor confronts the marble block, which heads the sequence of reliefs: it is the "Greyhound," Dante's image for the one who would save Italy from its ruinous state, Henry of Luxembourg; for Terragni, Mussolini.

A significant discrepancy between the model and the drawings requires note. The model includes a low wall at the rear of the building, which blocks the view to the entry hall and provides a passage, at the top of a short stair, to the library (*figure 19*). The reason for its exclusion from the drawings is obvious: it would have marred a reading of the generating rectangles and squares of the composition. The difficulty in accommodating a rather banal and pragmatic element underscores the spiritual purity of idealized geometric shapes. The presence of one of the thirty-three glass columns of the Paradise, where one assumes a wall ought to be, also points to Terragni's struggle to resolve number and form.

The *Relazione sul Danteum* is an extraordinary document. It was written in an artificially florid style (even for Terragni), in apparent imitation of Mussolini, complete with repetition, overstatement, even non sequiturs, all of which would have impressed the Duce. Although Terragni may have written the document to "sell the product," it is unlikely that an architect of Terragni's talent and a true believer in fascism would create a building so full of meanings, correspondences, and refer-

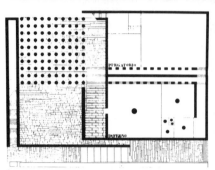

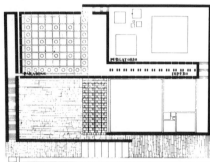

16 Danteum. Plan at 6 meters above the street, level two.

17 Danteum. Plan at 10 meters above the street, top level.

34

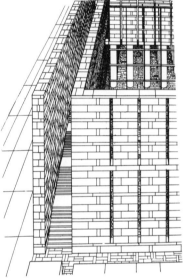

18 Danteum. Perspective, showing the final descent from Paradise, on axis with the block of marble representing the Greyhound.

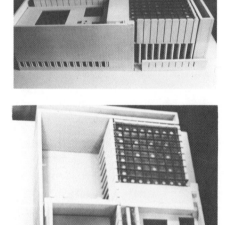

19 Danteum. Model views. The library windows are the only windows on vertical walls in the building.

ences unless he thought that they were all important. We must read the *Relazione* as if he meant every word.

My search into specific references from the *Relazione* text and from the building is an attempt to discern the meaning of the events, objects, and personages cited by Terragni — a Comasco intellectual and devout practicing Catholic living under fascism. For while he tells us a great deal, Terragni leaves enough unsaid as to elicit speculation about his deeper, even unconscious, intentions.

1. Shapiro, "Gruppo 7 Manifesto."
2. The term *rationalism*, despite Le Corbusier's attempt to prevent its widespread use (see his admonition to Sartoris of 1931, republished in Banham's *Theory and Design in the First Machine Age* [New York: Praeger, 1970]) remains the standard Italian term for modern architecture between the wars. *Rational*, or *rationalistic*, may carry a positive or negative connotation, in much the same way that the term *modernistic* weighs negatively in English architectural jargon.
3. Giulio Carlo Argan, in the theme speech at the Terragni Congress, Sept. 1968, in *L'Architettura* (May 1969), 6–7.
4. The hollowness of fascist town planning is eloquently expressed in the report of the completion of Saubaudia, one of the new towns in the reclaimed Pontine Marshes. See *Architettura* (1935). The building typology and the layout of Saubaudia reveal that the primary function of this town was as a theater for Mussolini's displays and harangues. The architects were indeed faithful to their clients' needs.
5. Piacentini either designed or judged in competition nearly all the major buildings erected for the regime, including the Florence Railway Station, the University City in Rome, the Via della Conciliazione (in front of St. Peters in Rome), the Town Center of Brescia, and the Plan of E'42 (now the EUR district in Rome). Upon Piacentini's death in 1960, Zevi wrote an obituary headline that read "Piacentini Died in 1925."
6. See Marcello Piacentini, *L'Architettura d'Oggi* (Roma: Paolo Cremonese, 1930); and Piacentini, various articles republished in Luciano Patetta, *L'Architettura in Italia, 1919–1943, Le Polemiche* (Milano: CLUP, 1972).
7. The word *colonna* refers to those columns used in the classical orders. Columns as simple static support are called *pilastri*. The differences in language are, of course, typical to the development of the concepts, and the existence of the distinction underscores the perceived cultural directive toward classicism in Italy in the twenties and thirties. See Ugo Ojetti, "Lettera a Marcello Piacentini," *Pegaso* 1933, in Patetta, *L'Architettura.*

8. Piacentini displayed a seemingly schizophrenic division between his writings and his taste in buildings, as noted by some scholars, particularly Zevi, who called Piacentini a "quick-change artist" in his latest edition of *Storia dell'Architettura Moderna* (Torino: Einaudi, 1975).
9. I find interesting parallels between this position of almost fifty years ago and Kenneth Frampton's ideals, based on Ahrendt, in *Oppositions* 4, "On Reading Heidegger" (Oct. 1974), editorial statement.
10. The actual wording was, "I don't say that there ought to be two architectures ... one in underwear and one in evening dress." From Patetta, *L'Architettura* (author's trans.), 161. There is no doubt he meant that there *ought* to be such a symbolic division.
11. Until recently the work of Peter Eisenman has been the major source in English for discussion about Terragni. Eisenman stresses Terragni's tendency to abstract elements into a code of formal relationships. See Peter Eisenman, "From Object to Relationship I," *Casabella* 344 (Jan. 1970), and "From Object to Relationship II," *Perspecta* (no. 13–14, 1971), 36–65. Eisenman's contribution to understanding Terragni cannot be overemphasized. His work has brought Terragni out from under the Corbusian-Miesian perception, to where Terragni's work can be appreciated in its own right. Zevi's analysis of the Casa del Fascio in Como also stresses abstraction: see *Storia dell'Architettura.*
12. Quoted in Corrado Maltese, *Arte Moderna in Italia, 1785–1943* (Torino: Einaudi, 1962), 423.
13. Enrico Mantero, *Giuseppe Terragni e la Città del Razionalismo in Italia* (Rome: Dedalo, 1969), 130. Terragni also defended international modern architecture against charges of Bolshevism and "Jewishness," but did so in terms of style, not the liberal social leanings of the movement.
14. According to Luigi Zuccoli, Terragni's assistant from the Novocumum to the end of his life, Terragni was a devout Catholic and a bit of a mystic. Sundays he would travel to the periphery of Como to hear

36

mass in the unfrequented medieval church of S. Abbondio so as to be alone and quiet. His identification with Dante must be seen in this light. From my interview with Zuccoli, March 1976.

15. From "Statuto per il Danteum," Archivio Centrale Dello Stato.

16. The Inferno was begun in April 1932 and presented to Mussolini in 1936. In February 1937 Valdameri informed Mussolini that the Purgatory was complete. The entire volume was given to Mussolini in an audience on 9 February 1938. (See *Il Messaggero,* 12 February 1938; from Archivio Centrale dello Stato, Doc. 509, 374, Segretaria Particolare del Duce. Most information concerning Valdameri, the Danteum Project Commission, and its history comes from these documents.) Valdameri contributed a total of 4,500,000 lire for the publication of the *Commedia.*

17. See letter dated 19 October 1938 from Valdameri to Osvaldo Sebastiani, Special Secretary to Mussolini (contained in Busta 609, 374, above). The correspondence for the Danteum is reprinted in Documents, below.

18. There is no written documentation on Mussolini's reaction. For this I am indebted to Signora Editta Lingeri, who stated that her husband returned to Milan elated over the reaction of the Head of State. She also related a charming story of how her husband had stepped on the Duce's foot during the presentation. Characteristically, Mussolini shrugged it off in good humor and high spirits. The exact date of the model construction is also uncertain, but Luigi Zuccoli, Terragni's assistant, and Piercarlo Lingeri, Pietro's son, believe that the model was made after the drawings were completed.

19. From "Statuto del Danteum."

20. See Henry Millon, "The Role of History of Architecture in Fascist Italy," *Journal of the Society of Architectural Historians* (March 1965), 53–58.

21. See chap. 2, below, concerning the site for the Danteum, the first site chosen for the Palazzo Littorio competition.

22. "Statuto del Danteum."

23. See Patetta, *L'Architettura,* for reprints of the great debate between Ojetti and Piacientini concerning Italian "character" and "arches and columns."

24. See Documents.

25. Giuseppe Terragni, *Relazione sul Danteum,* unpublished manuscript (1938), para. 20 (see chap. 4, below).

26. See Renzo de Felice, *Intervista sul Fascismo* (Rome: Laterza and Figli, 1975). De Felice argues that M. Sarfatti influenced Mussolini in terms of the ancient empire.

27. See Documents for complete text of Bontempelli's letter.

28. See chap. 5, below.

29. When I first began research on the Danteum project I believed it to be a collaboration between Terragni and Lingeri in relatively equal measure; similar, therefore, to their collaboration on the Milan Apartment Houses of the thirties. By the time I finished this book I was convinced that the generative ideas for the project were those of Terragni. I am still convinced of that. In this volume I have tried to be impartial toward various collaborators, yet one must always consider authorship, even when the object in question is more recent than the Danteum, and memories and documents more accessible.

The importance of my research is not specific attribution of authorship but the design process of an architect. This book concerns Terragni and *his* ideas of architectural meaning and form. The Danteum is the vehicle for the explanation of those ideas. I trust that the various texts and footnote references explain my views and give proper credit to those who deserve it, particularly to Pietro Lingeri, whose individual work stands to document his creative gifts.

30. These are the recollections of the Lingeri family. The design development of the project bears the Lingeri style, making it impossible to determine with any accuracy the authorship of the building. Lingeri was always concerned with the rigors of the plan, while Terragni often concerned himself with the facade. Thus one must attribute a good deal of the final Danteum design to Lingeri. It is my opinion, based on Terragni's other work and on the sketches, that he was the moving force behind the Danteum. There is also a subtle

hint to this in the way in which the correspondence concerning the project is written, always placing Terragni's name first rather than in the alphabetical order common in Fascist Italy. See Documents below. This is to correct an erroneous footnote in my article "Quando Terragni Parlava con Dante," *Parametro* 46 (May 1976), in which I stated that Editta and Piercarlo Lingeri had said that Terragni designed the Danteum.

31. *Relazione*, para. 7.
32. *Ibid.*, para. 3.
33. *Ibid.*, para. 10.
34. *Ibid.*, para. 11.
35. *Ibid.*
36. See chap. 4, the sequence of photos of an imagined promenade, supplemented by tercets of the *Comedy*.
37. *Relazione*, para. 13.
38. *Ibid.*
39. *Ibid.*, para. 10.
40. *Ibid.*, para. 11.
41. *Ibid.*, para. 10.
42. *Ibid.*
43. *Ibid.*
44. The authorship of the figures is uncertain, although they vaguely resemble the work of Sironi.
45. *Relazione*, para. 9.
46. *Ibid.*
47. *Ibid.*, para. 23.
48. *Ibid.*
49. *Ibid.*
50. *Ibid.*, para. 25.
51. *Ibid.*
52. *Ibid.*, para. 26.
53. *Ibid.*, para. 28.
54. *Ibid.*, para. 8.
55. *Ibid.*, para. 12 and 13.

Nor creator, nor creature, my son,
was ever without love, either natural
or rational ... the natural is always
without error; but the other may err
through an evil object, or through too
little or too much vigour.
Dante, Purgatory, *Canto XVII*

TERRAGNI AND HIS SOVRCES

I DO NOT INTEND TO ARGUE HERE THAT THE DAN-
teum represents a pinnacle of Terragni's career and that all
his previous work can be viewed as a prelude. Yet there
are qualities in Terragni's work that appear up to and
beyond 1938 that seem to me to gain their most explicit
expression in the Danteum. I feel it necessary, therefore, to explain the
work of Terragni that is precursory to the Danteum project, making the
project less of an anomaly than it first appears.

A discussion of Terragni's sources and the way he transformed them
into architecture is an appropriate introduction to the Danteum.
Throughout his artistic career Terragni depended on received images of
various kinds, to the point where he was accused of plagiarism more
than once. [1] Lorenzo Rocchi has called him " ... an able eclectic, col-
lecting a pile of disparate references.... " [2] While I would not reduce
Terragni's oeuvre to such simple terms, it is true that from the Officina
per la Produzione del Gas (1927) to the Distribuzione di Benzina Standardizzato (1940) he collected architectural themes upon which to
make variations, using several sources for a number of transformations.

Terragni handled his source material beginning with the direct imitation of detail forms, moving to the adaptation of plan and *parti*
forms, then to the inclusion of "found objects," without regard to scale

or function, finally arriving at the adaptation of geometric ordering systems unrelated to human activity or static structural systems. Accompanying this formal development, which is not strictly chronological (some of his last works are derivative in terms of corporeal form), is a development of symbolic content, which by contrast does follow a chronological pattern. Terragni's symbolic content emerged as the creation of architectural metaphors of modern materials and techniques in imitation of the new architecture of northern Europe; it then shifted (circa 1932) to the display of fascist ideas of various kinds, and ultimately turned to a more general cultural-historical-literary mode of expression.

The Danteum is one instance of the convergence of source as geometric order with a cultural-historical-literary symbolic content. As such it is perhaps the most independent and original statement of any of Terragni's buildings or projects, qualities underscored by the fact that the building cannot be typecast as either rationalist or monumentalist. Nor is it a simple compromise between these two extremes of polemic and style.

The Officina per la Produzione del Gas (1927) (*figure 20*) resembles the Bauhaus complex (*figure 21*) of the previous year, with its massing and composition expressed in the pinwheel plan and functional specificity of each wing, as if the elements of some technical program had determined their shapes and structural systems. The romanticism of Terragni's structural imagery is also reminiscent of the Russian work with which he had come into contact through magazines. Like any constructivist work — Lissitzsky's Lenin podium, for example — the Officina displays a somewhat implausible structural system, which is intended as a metaphor of the conditions producing modern steel structures. The Officina project is further a collage of modern architectural forms. It contains an oddly shaped pavilion on *pilotis* in the manner of Le Corbusier; a loft-space closed by a vaulted roof contained within a rectangular volume, recalling the work of Behrens; a low wing with a rounded corner, like the early buildings of Mendelsohn; and a water tank carried on a cruciform support, recalling anonymous engineering works.

The most famous of Terragni's alleged adaptations are the Casa del Fascio in Como (1932–1936) and the Novocumum Apartments in Como (1927–1929). Ironically these works are less derivative than

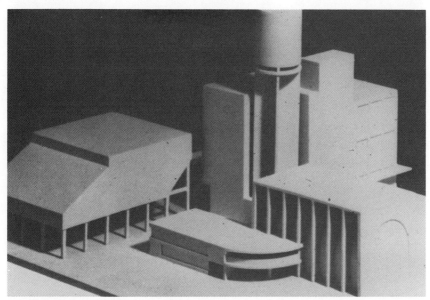

20 Terragni, Officina per la produzione del gas
(Gas Works project), 1927.

21 Gropius, Bauhaus, Dessau, 1926. Model.

most of Terragni's projects and buildings. The Novocumum block derives more from a response to the adjacent building on the site (*figure 22*) than from a reading of Golossov's Zuiev Club of the previous year.[3] The Casa del Fascio in Como (*figures 23 and 24*) is patently a Renaissance palace *before* it is a version of the "Vesna" school in Brno (*figure 25*) or the Nursing Home in Kassel (*figure 26*), the two buildings Terragni was accused of plagiarizing, as de Seta has noted. [4] As late as 1941 Piacentini published a comparison of Terragni's Casa del Floricoltore in Rebbio, the Schroder house in Utrecht, and a house by Antonin Raymond in Tokyo, implying that forms of the modern style were being passed around without regard to context. [5]

44

At Erba, Terragni designed a monument using classical forms (1927–1932) (*figures 27, 28, 29*), similar to some of his tombs. This tendency to couple "modern" style with more traditional elements and styling has led Rocchi to propose a split in Terragni's artistic personality, supporting " ... the idea that the monument of Erba, the Tomba Stecchini, the Albergo Posta Hotel, the Tomba Pirovano, the Danteum, the Casa del Fascio at Lissone, are products of the *right* hand of Terragni, the autocratic and fascist hand, while all the other works are of the *left* hand, international and 'European' [my italics]." [6] The Danteum, however, more likely lies in the "center," not on the "right," even if one accepts Rocchi's oversimplification.

Terragni's reliance on classical detail rather than classical organization seems to have ebbed in the early thirties. [7] He soon came to adhere exclusively to the detailed language of modern forms, if not always to modern ideas and free-plan organization, like early Mies or Le Corbusier.

Perhaps the most directly derived of Terragni's buildings is the winning entry for the Scuola Media competition in Busto Arsizio (1934) (*figure 30*). In this project Terragni borrowed a motif from a building at the University of Bern, which had been published in *Architettura* two years before (*figure 31*). [8]

22 Terragni, Novocumum Apartments, Como, 1927–1929. The upper floors of the adjacent building date from long after both buildings were built. The block is completed by the curved ends.

23 Terragni, Casa del Fascio, Como, 1932–1936. Photo taken during construction.

24 Terragni, Casa del Fascio, Como, 1932–1936. Photomontage with "graffiti."

25 V. Fuchs, School in Brno, Czechoslovakia, 1928. Photo is from the Terragni studio in Como.

26 O. Haesler and K. Wolker, Old Age Home, Kassel, Germany, 1932. Photo is from the Terragni studio in Como.

27 Terragni, Monument to the fallen, Erba, 1927–1932. Preliminary drawings. (Drawing #0100 according to the number system developed by Attilio Terragni after WWII.)

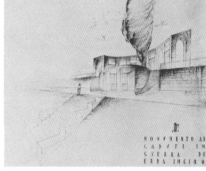

28 Terragni, Monument to the fallen, Erba. Photo. Note the influences of Muzio and the Novecento style.

29 Terragni, Monument to the fallen, Erba. Perspective sketch. Terragni's abstraction emerges.

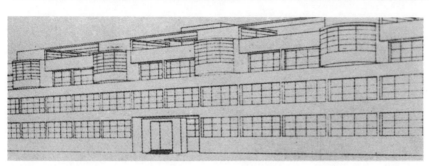

30 Terragni, High school project, competition in
Busto Arsizio, 1934.

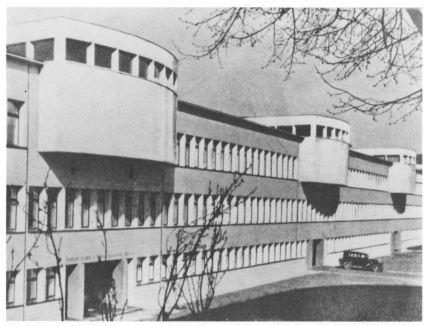

31 Salvisberg and Brechbuhl, Building at the
University of Bern, 1932. This photo was published in *Architettura*, 1932.

A T THE SAME TIME TERRAGNI WAS AT WORK ON the Casa del Fascio. The building resembles an ideal Renaissance palazzo (*figure 32*), complete with courtyard, front-back facade distinctions, and *piano nobile*. The model of the palazzo, exemplified by the Palazzo Farnese (*figure 33*), is used further in the circulation system of the building, which displays not only the typical axis/cross-axis layout but also a standard stair location. The stair leads to the *piano nobile* and the major room of the Casa in the manner of its model. The traditional qualities of this building are masked partially by a complex and intricate facade perhaps unparalleled in the modern movement, where a variety of fenestration is integrated within a frame system in the image of modern construction. The scheme of stripping away at the surface of the facade (*figure 34*) places Terragni closer to Renaissance architects, for example, than to a modernist such as Le Corbusier, whose buildup of the facade from the cantilevered floor slab outward is the inverse of Terragni's motif.

Closer to the ideas of Le Corbusier is Terragni and Lingeri's Casa Toninello in Milan of 1933 (*figure 35*). This building closely resembles Le Corbusier's Maison Plainex (1927) (*figure 36*) in that the volumetric expression denies the reality of the plan and makes a gesture toward the scale and rhythmic divisions of the building existing in the street. The lateral dimensions of the context buildings are repeated on the tripartite facades of both Plainex and Toninello, and both buildings contain projections that line up with an adjacent facade, leaving a shallow zone of semiprivate space as a visual transition. In the Maison Plainex and the Casa Toninello the spaces behind the taut plane of the facade are *not* the symmetrical spaces implied by the facade expression. In the tradition of the Parisian Hotel, Le Corbusier developed an idealized facade relating to the street and determined by the necessities of expression of the concrete frame. It was a *tour de force* of modernism, and the adaptation by Terragni and Lingeri incorporated the same expression of construction. In addition, the plan of the Casa Toninello recalls that of Maison Plainex, reflecting the same organization of functions and location of stair (*figures 37 and 38*).

Perhaps the most important of Terragni's unbuilt projects is the Palazzo Littorio Competition Solution *A* (1934), designed in collaboration with Lingeri, Vietti, Carminati, Saliva, and the painters Nizzoli and

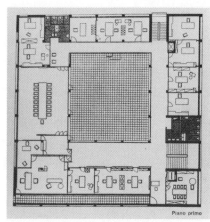

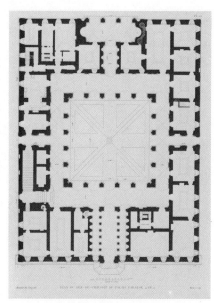

32 Terragni, Casa del Fascio, Como. Plan of the second floor.

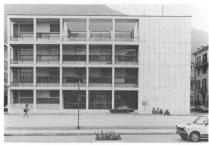

34 Terragni, Casa del Fascio, Como. Facade.

33 Antonio da Sangallo, Palazzo Farnese, Rome, begun 1515. Plan of the second floor. The format and development of the plan is repeated in the Casa del Fascio.

49

50

36 Le Corbusier, Maison Plainex, Paris, 1927. Front facade.

35 Terragni and Lingeri, Casa Toninello, Milano, 1934. Front facade.

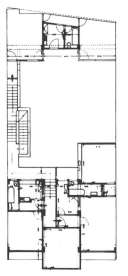

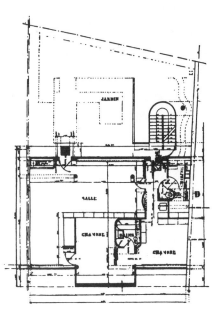

37 Terragni and Lingeri, Casa Toninello. Plan.   38 Le Corbusier, Maison Plainex. Plan.

Sironi. [9] The scheme is a combination of modern and antique motifs integrated in a manner uncharacteristic of the modern movement, even in Italy.

The Palazzo Littorio was to be sited in the Via dell'Impero in Rome, the site later chosen for the Danteum, and the character of the archaeological zone was an important design determinant for both projects, four years apart. The street was a recent addition to Mussolini's Rome and to a great degree symbolized both the new archaeological interest in antiquity and the imperial pretensions of the so-called fascist revolution. It was inaugurated in 1932 for the first decade of that revolution, and connected Piazza Venezia (the location of Mussolini's headquarters and his seat of power) with the Colosseum, the largest surviving monument of antiquity. The street covered most of the Imperial Fora, forming an urban edge to the Republican Forum and, for the first time since antiquity, the Basilica of Maxentius and Constantine was completely liberated from a base of rubble and houses that had hidden nearly one quarter of its height (*figure 39*).

The Basilica was indeed an important component in the formal and symbolic program of the competition. Marcello Piacentini, who wrote the competition brief, advised the entrants to relate their designs to the Basilica by keeping all building forms lower than the top of that monument, "except those forms needed for aesthetic purposes." [10] Necessary elements presumably would be those like the normally requisite *torre Littorio.*

The program for this competition involved much more than space requirements, and strong feelings about what architectural style to use on this site were expressed in the Chamber of Deputies. Typical of the arguments in the *Camera* was this: "On the Via dell'Impero we must walk with caution, because there passes the entire Roman civilization (loud applause) ... we must not place on the Via dell'Impero the Florence Railway Station." [11]

This was a clear, antirationalist statement that referred to the winning scheme of Michelucci and his collaborators for the Florence Station, an admonition to the competitors that the *Camera* would not look with favor on architecture it considered "bolshevik" or "German" (Germany was still, in 1934, Italy's adversary).

39 Basilica of Maxentius, Rome. On the low wall
are reliefs made in the 1930s of the development
of the Roman Empire. The last relief, showing
the New Roman Empire, was removed after 13
July 1943.

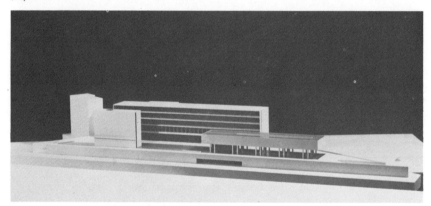

40 BBPR with Figini and Pollini, Palazzo Littorio
competition, 1934. Model. An overtly modern
building, it stood no chance of winning.

Like a barometer of architectural sentiment in Fascist Italy, the resulting entries reflected a division of style into traditional and modern, "Roman" and "international," with each project seeking to summarize the glory of fascism. A solution like the one submitted by the BBPR group (Banfi, Belgioiosi, Peressutti, and Rogers) with Figini and Pollini (*figure 40*), the most "international" of all the entries, was doomed from the start, not so much because the fascist hierarchy was against modern architecture, but rather because a modern building would have seemed out of place in the context. This argument was by no means the exclusive property of fascist or Nazi reaction; it surfaced in almost every country, democracies included. Even the newspapers voiced opinion; in *La Sera* of 28 May 1934, the antirationalist polemic was hurled:

> We are all in accord: the Casa Littorio is a "Monumental Building" of "Public use," spiritual: it is a commemorative building, one of celebration; it represents an idea; it must always render that idea in a real and actual manner, across time. It is the idea of our history. Therefore the Casa Littoria...must refute the industrial and commercial forms of "Rationalism.".[12]

Terragni and his collaborators felt these conditions intensely. Explaining their intention to "recreate with pure forms (rectangle and circle) the urbanistic quality of the zone, shown in the plan of 1:100," the architects began by choosing a base map that contained the ancient and the modern contexts. [13] They were the only team to do so. Onto the large site plan they pasted an aerial view of the project site (taken from the competition program) and two illustrations of ancient works: the complex at Tyrins in the time of the Mycenean civilization and the ancient Egyptian temple of Isis in Philae, containing Roman ruins as well. Tyrins was to illustrate a building complex of diverse elements unified by a single theme — the girdling wall — that would correspond conceptually to the enormous facade of the Palazzo Littorio scheme. The Temple at Philae was included for its huge pylon wall, through which one passes to the sanctuary. The equivalent in the Palazzo Littorio is the passage through the pylon facade, through which Mussolini would walk, silhouetted against the sky, on his way to deliver his public speeches.

Pasted onto the smaller site plan was a series of illustrations of ancient architecture, intended to explain the architects' use of historical
principles and concepts (*figures 41, 42, 43, 44*). The architects went to
a great deal of trouble assembling this collage of images and adding captions to the examples. The captions explain specific formal properties of
scale, configuration, and relationships of geometry that Solution *A*
shared with its ancient counterparts.

From left to right the illustrations are a collage of Roman buildings;
an ancient tomb from Egypt; a grouping of unidentified ancient (and
primitive) sacred spaces; the Acropolis at Athens; a baroque stair in section; the facade of the Parthenon; the temple of Poseidon at Paestum;
the plan of a Roman theater; and a Choisy drawing of a Roman vault.
A brief caption accompanies each illustration and explains how it was
chosen as an example of ancient architecture that creates monumentality
and harmony; the captions imply that this can be achieved in a modern
idiom as well, if the underlying principles are understood.

The specific captions are significant. The caption for the Roman
Collage reads, "Example of the joining of round and rectangular
forms," relating it to the form of the "Sacrario" of the Palazzo Littorio.

The Egyptian Tomb has the caption, "One arrives at the crypt
across a gallery: spiritual preparation," like the Roman Collage.

The grouping of ancient and primitive sacred places is explained as
the "superimposition of the cylinder and cube, bringing the notion into
three dimensions."

The Acropolis at Athens is an example of the site-planning concept:
"Urbanism of pure forms disposed according to the sun. Note the relation of the temples as regards the Propylea. The form of the Greek
theater was given a grand artistic effect with its crescent to the whole
composition."

The Baroque Stair is noted for its "parallel stairs closed between
two walls; the steps are very high."

The diagram of the facade of the Parthenon at Athens shows how
the Greeks made visual adjustments to "the horizontal and vertical
lines" to correct for misreadings of curvature and straight edges. A
similar effect appears in the facade of the Palazzo Littorio *A,* where,
from below, the upper edge of the facade would be perceived as
straight, rather than concave.

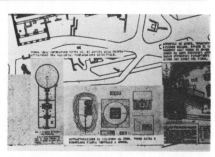

41 Terragni, Lingeri, Carminati, Saliva, Vietti, Sironi, and Nizzoli, Palazzo Littorio competition, 1934, Scheme *A*. Site plan detail showing a collage of ancient Roman plans.

42 Palazzo Littorio, Scheme *A*. Site plan detail showing ancient Egyptian tombs and various primitive buildings. The theme of the circle in the square is reflected in the plan of Terragni's project.

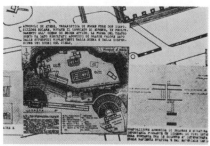

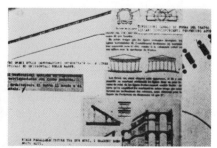

43 Palazzo Littorio, Scheme *A*. Site plan detail of the Acropolis at Athens.

44 Palazzo Littorio, Scheme *A*. Site plan detail of adjustments to the facade of the Parthenon.

45 Palazzo Littorio, Scheme *A*. Model of complete ensemble: Palazzo Littorio, Colosseum, Basilica of Maxentius across the Street of the Empire.

The Roman Theater resembles the Sala dei 1000 in the Palazzo and carries the caption, "Ideal conditions for the Roman Theater."

"Italian construction" begins the caption for the temple of Poseidon at Paestum. It exemplifies the monumental scale achieved through the enormous steps of the stylobate.

The Choisy drawing of a Roman vault illustrates ancient construction; its spatial hierarchy enabled the Romans to create "horizontal buildings and eliminate in the plan any errors in central focus" by embedding high spaces on a long building, exactly the theme of spatial hierarchy in Palazzo Littorio A.

One of the most obvious characteristics of the historical collage is its debt to Le Corbusier, particularly to *Towards a New Architecture*. In 1926–1927 the Gruppo Sette, with Terragni as its spokesman, took Le Corbusier's text as a point of departure for the important themes and basic principles of all periods of architecture. For the Palazzo Littorio, Terragni and his collaborators again mirrored Le Corbusier's facility to abstract constants, but with the added symbolic overtones of a monumentality appropriate for the Fascist State. The architects' report and illustrations accurately explained the building complex. Their desire was to

> gather into *one* project [the lower half of the composition] the major [existing] characteristics of an environment that is intelligently and moderately interpreted, leaving to the other [upper] project the task of stabilizing the higher level of modernity that was made possible through the union of our powers and ideas.[14]

This contextual approach led to the replication of the ancient context on the ground, with a modern design on top. The concave facade (*figure 45*), hung on two huge trusses, symbolized modernity, a rhetorical gesture that does not enclose internal space, but rather suggests the "arms" of Bernini's colonnades in Piazza San Pietro.

To further match the existing context the architects aligned their buildings with the "axis of the Forum of Trajan," a relationship that could not have been understood by anyone without reference to the plan itself, but which was nonetheless important to Terragni and his partners. [15]

This sort of historical reference reemerged in the Danteum design with a more subtle expression. There is no doubt that Terragni's memory of the Palazzo Littorio Solution *A* influenced his design of the Danteum. However, in the Palazzo Littorio the traditional design method and group of motifs is not confined to the ground plane (*figure 46*). All the major spaces, for example, are arranged axially, within a carefully layered system reminiscent of Palladian villas or Rainaldian church plans. While the overall composition might owe something to Le Corbusier's Salvation Army Building in Paris (1930), the axis/cross-axis arrangement found in the Palazzo Littorio organizes the rooms of the Sala dei 1000, the Sacrario, and the Duce (*figure 47*). This plan surfaces in the early schemes for the project and at least in one of Terragni's sketches (*figure 48*), in which the separation of volumes is partially suppressed in favor of more classical forms — a podium and courtyard — leading to the apsidal volume (presumably the Sala dei 1000). The cross-axis in this early scheme displays a figural volume resembling the Sacrario of the final version.

The final version of Solution *A* reveals an insistent massing of "separate blocks of buildings corresponding to the program" [16] and the project's modernistic structural expressionism, recalling the Officina per la Produzione del Gas. The most revealing statement for the separation of the building masses was the intention that "the Round Sacrario be volumetrically removed from the exhibit [of the Revolution] and submerged in the soil of Imperial Rome." [17] Within this exhibit space was inserted a wall in the shape of a question mark, imitating the retaining wall across the street, which was unearthed along with the Basilica of Maxentius. This wall can be read in the plan as another means to enhance the symmetry across the Via dell'Impero. It is also an attempt to identify the Palazzo with the Basilica — an important symbol of the origins of Christianity — within the context of ancient Rome.

The project's ground-plan organization, plan motifs, and spaces combine to create a scheme that is indistinguishable from the ancient context underfoot, making a symbolic and literal correspondence between ancient and modern, a correspondence that the reactionary architects in Fascist Italy, with all their *Romanità*, were unable to accomplish.

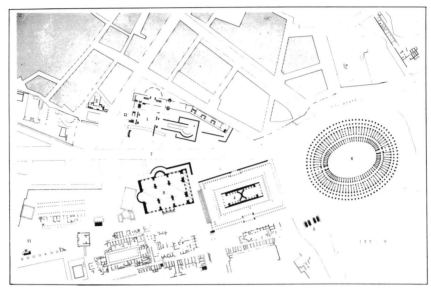

46 Palazzo Littorio, Scheme *A*. Plan of the
ground floor. The symmetry across the street
would not be perceived without a reading of the
plan.

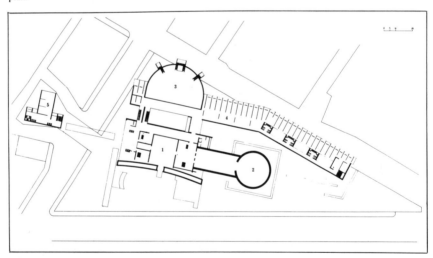

47 Palazzo Littorio, Scheme *A*. Plan of the
fourth floor. The Duce is on the main axis, the
"Sacrario" on the cross-axis.

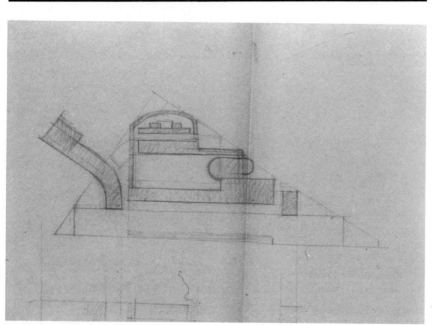

48 Terragni, Preliminary sketch for the Palazzo
Littorio, 1933.

BY 1934–1935 TERRAGNI HAD BEGUN ANOTHER kind of transformation of formal subject matter, one dependent on a greater degree of abstraction from the "real" and concrete conditions of an architectural problem. In 1932 he began a collaboration with Mario Radice who, at about the same time, had begun to develop his own abstract style of painting as an avowed synthesis of Mondrian and purism (*figure 49*). [18] Soon afterward the motif of the displaced rectangle began to appear in Terragni's sketches and projects, in both plan and section. In the Casa del Floricoltore in Rebbio, Terragni's preliminary sketches were so close to Radice's drawings of the same period that they might be mistaken for the work of a single artist (*figures 50 and 51*).

In this project and others immediately following, Terragni adapted a two-dimensional system of organizing shapes and colors on canvas to the three-dimensional world of architectural form. The importance of this adaptation was the lack of pictorial or spatial similarity between Radice's paintings and Terragni's sketches; there seems to be no reason in Terragni's system for such a relationship. His adaptation, therefore, was totally abstract and out of context. It was a springboard for the creative process.

During the period between the first Palazzo Littorio schemes (1934) and the Danteum (1938), Terragni experimented often with composition. The Casa del Floricoltore is a simplified version of the sketches, similar in plan (*figure 52*) to the Radice compositions of the period of the Casa del Fascio fresco (*figure 53*). However, the slipped rectangle motif did receive some architectonic purpose once it had been abstracted: the zones exposed in the process of slippage provided horizontal and vertical circulation. This scheme was used in the Danteum three years later and indeed, throughout the rest of Terragni's career; he abandoned the pragmatic rationale of circulation distribution only in his last major work, the Casa Giuliani-Frigerio (1939).

Sketches from this period record Terragni's aesthetic experimentation. As in his initial phase (Officina del Gas to Casa del Fascio in Como), Terragni now turned first to contemporary sources for his inspiration, internalizing them before he could synthesize an original statement. Whereas in the twenties he turned to Gropius and the

49 Mario Radice, *Composition CFO*, 1932–1934.
Combined purism and neoplasticism.

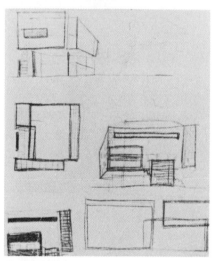

50 Terragni, House for a horticulturist, Rebbio
(Como), 1935–1937. Preliminary sketches. The
overlapping rectangle pervades.

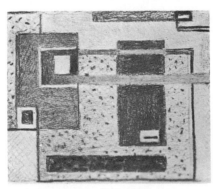

62

51 Radice, *Composition CFS*, 1934.

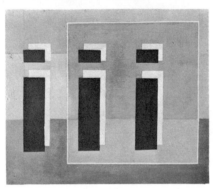

53 Radice, *Composition CF 120*, 1932–1935.

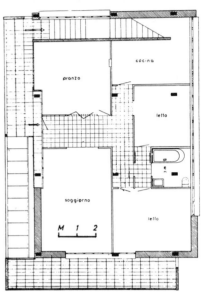

52 Terragni, House for a horticulturist, Rebbio. Plan. The overlapping rectangle motif combined with the golden section.

Russians, in the thirties Terragni used Le Corbusier's work directly as a source. His dependency on Corbusier is demonstrated in the first version of the Casa del Floricoltore, in its structural scheme (the Maison Dom-ino) and its rear elevation (the Villa Savoye) (*figure 54*).

Terragni was indebted to Le Corbusier for other projects, as well. In the Casa del Fascio, Rione Trastevere in Rome (1940) (*figure 55*), the motif of the displaced rectangle is similar to Le Corbusier's famous section of the first version of the Villa Carthage (1928) (*figure 56*). For the Stazione di Servizio Standardizzato (circa 1940), Terragni adapted Le Corbusier's canopy from the Liège Pavilion (1937) (*figure 57*), published in the 1939 *Oeuvre Complète*. (The first of Le Corbusier's versions of this form was the Nestlè Pavilion, 1928.)

The preliminary scheme for the Villa at Carthage is found in Terragni's sketches of uncertain date, possibly for a villa in Portofino (1936) but conceivably for the Casa del Floricoltore. This particular sheet of sketches (#0247) (*figure 58*) contains sections and elevations resembling the Villa Carthage section combined with the diagonal stair volume of the Maison Citrohan, and displaying a Corbusian separation of structure and enclosure indicated by the single-line columns.

In the Villa sul Lago (1936) Terragni created his only Corbusian *plan libre* building (*figure 59*). The specific referents for the Villa sul Lago are the Villa Savoye and the Villa Stein, but the most Corbusian aspect of this project is simply its "ocean-liner" *parti,* with a promenade deck that circumvents the block of the building and an entrance over a gangplank. The constant rhythm of round columns and the unidirectional cantilever recall the Maison Dom-ino and the Villa Savoye; its curved wall presents its convex side to the living room and concave side to the dining room, reminiscent of the Villa Stein and Mies van der Rohe's Tugendhat House. The most significant Corbusian feature is the architectural promenade, whose sequence begins as in the Villa Savoye, with the *porte-cochère* leading to the *piano nobile,* and finishes like the Villa Stein at Garches, where the visitor is forced back through the envelope of the volume.

The Villa sul Lago is composed of buildings within buildings. The block of solid interior space that resides within the roofed volume is subdivided and zoned according to a public-private division, while the promenade reveals these spaces in a sequence that traverses the volume

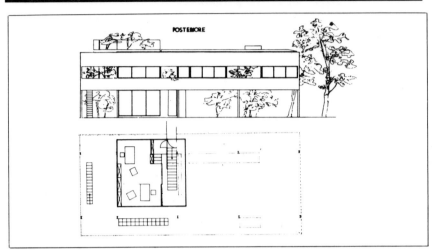

64

54 Terragni, House for a horticulturist, Rebbio. Preliminary plan and facade. A Corbusian scheme, later superseded by a more personal motif.

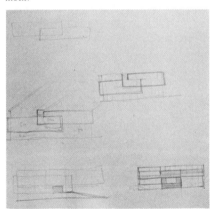

55 Terragni, Unbuilt project for Casa del Fascio, Rione Trastavere, Rome, 1940. Sketches.

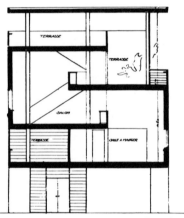

56 Le Corbusier, Villa at Carthage, first scheme, 1926. Section.

57 Le Corbusier, Liège Pavilion, 1938.

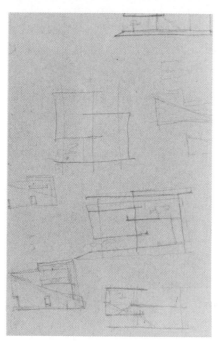

58 Terragni, Drawing #0247, possibly for a villa in Portofino. Le Corbusier's famous section makes its appearance.

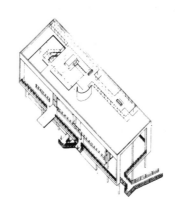

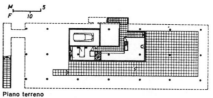

Piano terreno

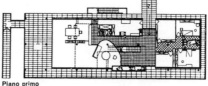

Piano primo

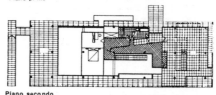

Piano secondo

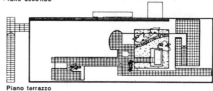

Piano terrazzo

59 Terragni, Villa on a Lake, project, 1936. Axonometric and plans. Terragni's most Corbusian project also resembles Mies's Tugendhat House.

lengthwise. This route further recalls the Maison La Roche (1923).
The interest in the sequence as counterpoint to the compositional
scheme is uncharacteristic of Terragni. The Casa del Floricoltore, the
Villa Bianca, and the Danteum rely on sequences of spaces organized
tightly around the geometric composition of elements, and the Casa del
Floricoltore is a direct source for the Danteum design. That is, the displacement of rectangles that generates the plan reveals the horizontal
and vertical circulation streams in the displaced, or leftover, zone (*figure
60*).

The above speculation is based on Terragni's constant reliance on
source material and on Le Corbusier's work in particular. The most
striking example of this infatuation is the sketch he made of Le Corbusier's project for a House for a College President (1935), outside Chicago, which had been published in the 1939 *Oeuvre Complète* (*figures 61
and 62*). Terragni's sketch is in the tradition of the Renaissance masters
who drew from their predecessors; it was his private note to himself
concerning an inspirational source, which ironically never appeared in
any of his buildings or projects. Rather, the drawing seems more a
confirmation of the volumetric organization of a previous project, the
Cantonal Library of Lugano (1935).

Terragni reused his *own* motifs in a number of projects. He copied
himself as well as others, and the plan of the Casa del Floricoltore is
only one of many derivations. The second-round competition project
for the Palazzo Littorio displays a *torre Littorio* (*figure 63*) adapted from
Terragni's preliminary project for the Sarfatti Monument (1934–1935)
(*figure 64*). [19] The project underwent changes in the design process,
and it is conceivable that Terragni abandoned the first scheme for the
very reason that it too closely resembled a Lictor's tower, that common
element of fascist party buildings. [20]

The final version of the monument to Margherita Sarfatti's brother
became, in its turn, a source for yet another Terragni project, the Casa a
Gradoni, circa 1940. For this source we have a photo of the Sarfatti
Monument taped to the sketch of the Casa a Gradoni (*figure 65*). The
great differences in scale and function recall Le Corbusier's biomorphic
adaptation of a snail shell for his Museum of the Square Spiral.

If the Casa del Floricoltore can be cited as the initial compositional
source for the Danteum — the overlapping rectangles, also seen in

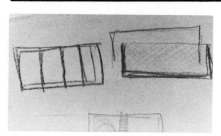

60 Terragni, Unnumbered sketches, possibly for the Danteum. Added to the square and golden section is a line of promenade.

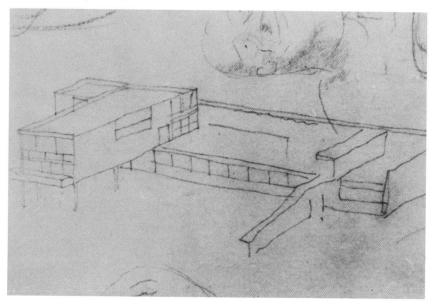

61 Terragni, Sketch after Le Corbusier's House for a college president. Perspective.

62 Le Corbusier, House for a college president, outside Chicago, 1935. Perspective.

63 Terragni, Palazzo Littorio competition, "Lictor's tower," second stage, 1937.

64 Terragni, Monument to Roberto Sarfatti, Colle Ercole, 1935. Preliminary sketch. The scale is different from the Palazzo Littorio, but the composition is the same.

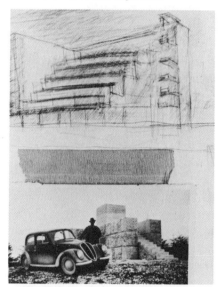

65 Terragni, Sketch for an apartment house in stepped section, with a photo of the monument to Roberto Sarfatti taped to it. Abstract form becomes the element that transcends function and size.

Radice's paintings — then the source for the cruciform scheme must be the competition entry for the Palazzo dei Congressi in E.U.R. (1937), designed with Lingeri and Cattaneo (*figure 66*). Terragni's preliminary sketches show the building organized on a quadrapartite scheme, which is expressed only vaguely in the final plan. In addition to these preliminary sketches, there are some sketches of questionable purpose resembling the Palazzo dei Congressi (*figure 67*). They include some versions of a quadrapartite form combined with a spiral or pinwheel, forecasting the final version of the Danteum.

Terragni was influenced heavily by the publication of Le Corbusier's *Oeuvre Complète 1934–1938* of 1939; the aforementioned sketch after the House for a College President is one instance of many. Among these are a scheme for a stadium resembling Le Corbusier's Stadium for 100,000 Spectators (1936–1937), and the project for the Stazione di Servizio e Benzina (1940), which resembles Le Corbusier's Liège Bata Pavillon of 1938. The most significant adaptation is a section of the scheme for the Casa del Fascio, Rione Trastevere, Rome (1940), which is an almost exact replica of Le Corbusier's Immeuble Type V-R (the section that was to become the generating scheme of all his Unités d'Habitation). The Casa Giuliani-Frigerio (1939–1940), for which Le Corbusier's work was clearly an inspiration, is the most significant of Terragni's buildings to come from this period.

Terragni remained receptive to contemporary influence until the end of his career. However, his projects toward the late thirties show two important tendencies aside from direct architectural reference. One is a greater reliance on abstract forms as source material; the other is a conscious wrestling with historical plans to combine them with overtly modern forms into an organic whole. *Part* of the impetus for this tendency may have been the introduction of the *Autarchia* into Italian life. In 1936, with Luigi Figini and Gino Pollini, Terragni and Lingeri designed a building for the Accademia di Brera in *struttura autarchica*. But the "high-tech" qualities of the Danteum's Paradise space make it unlikely that Terragni's concept of architectural form was significantly altered by his attitude toward natural materials. The development from the Casa del Fascio in Como, where the Renaissance palace was given a modern "treatment," to the Palazzo Littorio *A,* where modern forms were literally suspended over antiquity, to the Danteum, where a

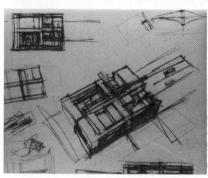 

66, 67 Terragni, Palazzo dei Ricevimenti e dei Congressi, Exposition of 1942, Rome, 1937. Sketches of various cruciform schemes.

dynamic and modernistic plan-form was then erected in traditional materials, chronicles Terragni's search for a constant, absolute, suprahistorical architecture.

We can divide Terragni's oeuvre into periods defined by his models. In the period from 1926 to 1932, German and Soviet architecture influenced him. From 1932 to 1936 (the period of the Casa del Fascio in Como) Terragni retrenched to traditional forms and *partis*, but overlaid these with his own notions of modern structure and abstract composition. From 1936 to 1938 he was influenced by abstract models and painting, culminating in the rigorous plan of the Danteum. It was during this period that Terragni began in earnest to use the square and the golden section as generating schemes. After 1938 he looked again to the modern movement, particularly to Le Corbusier, and ultimately created his richest building, the Casa Giuliani, the final plan of which also developed from the golden section.

1. For documentation of the plagiarism controversy over the Casa del Fascio in Como, see Mantero, *Giuseppe Terragni*.
2. In *L'Architettura* 163 (September 1969). Report by Lorenzo Rocchi.
3. *Ibid.*, report by Zuccoli.
4. Cesare de Seta, *La cultura architettonica in Italia tra le due Guerre* (Bari: Laterza, 1972), 169–246.
5. See "Strani Avvicinamenti," in *Architettura* (August 1941), 400–401.
6. Rocchi, *L'Architettura* 163 (May 1969).
7. There is some evidence that the classical Pirovano Tomb designed as late as 1936 was the work of Lingeri, not Terragni. This is the opinion of Piercarlo Lingeri, who stated that Terragni was no longer interested in work requiring classical "styling," and that he asked Lingeri to do the tomb.
8. See *Architettura* (October 1932), 568. Terragni was not alone in this derivation. A project by de Aquinega and Aizpurua for a secondary school in Cartagena, Spain (1932), also resembles the Bern University building by Salvisberg and Brechtbuhl. See George R. Collins, "Spain: A Case Study in Action and Reaction," *JSAH* (March 1965), 59–64.
9. There is some question as to who was the major influence on the various schemes for this project. Vietti remembers having originated the idea of the curved wall with the lines of stress inscribed on it, and that Terragni then developed the scheme. The volumetric distribution and plan organization is clearly Terragniesque.
10. See *Architettura*, Numero Speciale (1934), for the project documentation.
11. *La Sera*, 28 May 1934. Reprinted in Mantero, *Giuseppe Terragni*, 122–123.
12. *Ibid.*
13. *Ibid.*
14. *Ibid.*, 125.
15. *Ibid.*
16. *Ibid.*
17. *Ibid.*
18. See Guido Ballo, *Mario Radice* (Torino: ILTE, 1973), 23, 26.
19. For this observation I am indebted to Gabriele Milelli.
20. Terragni's reluctance to use the Lictor's tower in the Casa del Fascio in Como is documented by Diane Ghirardo in "The Politics of a Masterpiece: The Vicenda of Terragni's Casa del Fascio in Como," *The Art Bulletin*, vol. LXII, no. 3 (Sept. 1980), 466–478. Ironically, Terragni accepted the idea of the tower in his last public building, the Casa del Fascio in Lissone, 1940, realized with Antonio Carminati.

THE DANTEVM DESIGN

ONLY A FEW EXISTING SKETCHES BY TERRAGNI CAN be linked unquestionably to the Danteum project. These sketches show that he had conceived at least one scheme other than the final version, but there is no way of knowing for sure whether it predated the definitive project.

The major surviving sketch of what may be termed Scheme *A* reflects the preliminary gropings of the architect, including his notes to himself; Terragni raised questions about the nature of the building in these notes, six items listed on the drawing.

At the top he scribbled the words *"cultura Italiana di dolce stile novo,"* a reference to Dante's "sweet, gentle, smooth" reaction to rhetoric, a lyricism that blended elements and created textual ambiguities. Terragni might well have identified with Dante in this regard, having believed he superseded the "rhetoricism" of Muzio and the *Novecento* style, and integrated Italian lyricism with the northern rationalism of the International Style. Next he listed *"cultura pre-Dantesca (la notte del medioevo)"* (pre-Dantesque culture [literally, "the night of the Middle Ages"]), and here the image may describe the experience of Dante's enlightenment as parallel to Terragni's enlightenment under fascism. The call to "Virgilio" and "Roma," listed next, shows Terragni's need to connect the medieval Dante with the poet's ancient

Roman ancestry. Below this he indicated two design intentions: *"sulle facciate, tutti [sic] verse della D.C."* ("on the facade, all the verses of the *Divine Comedy"*), an idea that was quickly abandoned (presumably it was too blatant); and *"giunti dei blocchi,"* an enigmatic statement that suggests a variety of intentions. The "joints of the blocks" are the "glue" of the architectonic whole, the pragmatic structure made conceptual. This note was scribbled next to a sketch that resembled stone blocks in a slightly shifted joint pattern, similar to the motif of the shifted rectangle that Terragni used frequently. One of the versions of the Mambretti Tomb (*figure 68*) of early 1938 resembles this sketch, but in the plan of the Danteum Scheme *A* the shifted rectangle had yet to appear. This sketch is dated 25 February 1938; thus it is from roughly the same period of the beginning designs for the Danteum. There are no documents available attesting to the exact date of the commission.

The plan is composed of parallel walls that define building blocks, like lockers in a locker room or tombs in a *camposanto* (*figure 69*). The project resembles Le Corbusier's spiral museum project (1931) and Luciano Baldessari's Padiglione della Stampa (1933) at the Fifth Triennale (*figure 70*). This "locker-room scheme," as shown in the plan and a sketchy section (*figure 71*) (upon which are written the words *"fare Relazione Danteum"*), may also have been inspired by ancient Roman architecture, specifically the *sette sale* of the Golden House of Nero in Rome (*figure 72*). On the site plan that Terragni used for the Palazzo Littorio and the Danteum projects, there is a clear plan of the *sette sale;* it is possible that he recorded this image in his mind, to replay it in the design process of the Danteum. Although this argument is difficult to prove, other adaptations by Terragni indicate a similar process. Moreover, the *sette sale* was a source for the grottoes of the Renaissance, a period that Terragni held in esteem. The notion of continuity between ancient Rome and the Renaissance, and between the Renaissance and the modern era, constantly preoccupied Terragni and most of his contemporaries.

The Padiglione della Stampa, however, is the more plausible source, since this project and the Danteum deal with a prescribed route and promenade. The Danteum sketch in addition displays the lines of its route in a similar style to Baldessari's plan. The resulting scheme defines a corridor street system traversed by a sinuous route. The stair

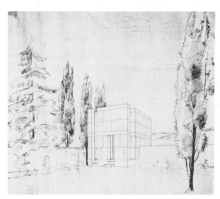

68 Terragni, Mambretti tomb, 1929 and 1938. Perspective.

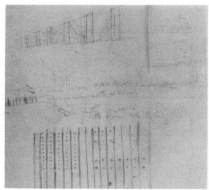

69 Terragni, Danteum, Scheme A. Sketches showing plan, perspective, a small section, and many handwritten notes.

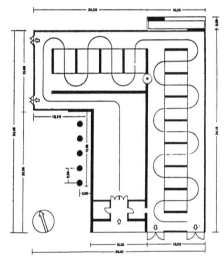

70 Luciano Baldesarri, Press Pavilion, V Triennale, Milan, 1933. Plan.

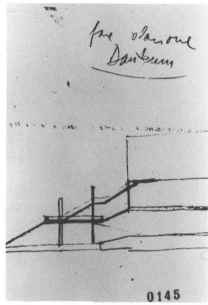

0145

71 Terragni, Section drawing, possibly for the Danteum. Above the sketch Terragni scribbled "Do the Danteum Relazione."

in the end bay plan is similar to the stair in the final design.

A small sketch of a section accompanies the plan and perspective (*figure 73*). It resembles the section of the final scheme and contains what appears to be a tall column in the space that becomes the entrance court in the final scheme. The word "Virgilio" appears attached to this column by a line. Perhaps Terragni was inclined initially toward a personification of architectural elements, with the column representing Virgil, Dante's guide through the Inferno and Purgatory. This leads to speculation that elements besides the marble block for the Veltro (Mussolini) may have encompassed such allegory.

The geometric organization that is so pervasive in the final Danteum design had not yet been developed at this early stage, but the numerical correspondences to the *Divine Comedy* that inform the final version are apparent in Scheme *A*.

In the *Comedy* the literary numerical divisions are three *cantiche* of thirty-three cantos each, plus one extra in the first *cantica*, making a total of one hundred cantos. The Poem is composed of three-line tercets; the first and third lines rhyme, the second line rhymes with the beginning of the next stanza, making a kind of overlap, reflected in the Danteum design. Dante describes the realms as having the following divisions: the Inferno is of nine levels, the vestibule makes the tenth. The Purgatory is of nine terraces, the terrestrial Paradise makes the tenth. Paradise is of nine heavens, Empyrean makes the tenth. Sinners in the Inferno are organized by three vices: Incontinence, Violence, and Fraud. Penitence is ordered on the basis of three types of natural love in Purgatory. Paradise is ordered on the basis of three types of Divine Love.

In Scheme *A* of the Danteum, five lines of ten circular columns, two lines of seven square columns, and two lines of three square columns all fit a Dantesque numerical breakdown. The square and the circle are important geometric forms for Dante and Terragni, and the choice of one over another was something about which Terragni obviously labored. In the *Relazione* he states that the circle would be the obvious choice for such a building, but that it had to be discarded because "the area it encloses is too modest for what was needed, but also because of the immediacy of potential conflict with the perfect and imposing ellipse of the Colosseum." [1]

ERRAGNI'S INSISTENCE ON GEOMETRIC AND mathematical correspondences to the *Comedy* combined with an adherence to geometry that derived, I believe, from three other sources: the displaced rectangle motif of the Casa del Floricoltore, the Basilica of Maxentius, and the Villa Stein at Garches by Le Corbusier.

Terragni's sketch #0250 (*figure 74*) shows various exercises in geometric patterns of overlapping squares and rectangles, and resembles the final Danteum design. The most consistent motif of the plan sketches on this sheet is the overlapping rectangle, drawn so as to reveal potential circulation through the scheme. The proportional system based on the golden rectangle finally made its appearance.

Another sketch (unnumbered) begins to explain the relationship of the slipped rectangle to the geometry of squares and rectangles that, as Terragni explained, derived from the Basilica of Maxentius across the street.

Terragni was careful to tell us that the Danteum proportions and dimensions (geometry and number, important Dantesque *separate* properties) were gleaned from the Basilica. What he omitted from the *Relazione* was that the slipped rectangle motif was derived as much from the Basilica of Maxentius as from his other sources. Further speculation reveals more correspondences between the Basilica and the Danteum.

The evidence begins with the sketches and is corroborated by the final design. The unnumbered sketch shows a scheme of overlap in a single direction alongside a scheme formed by two U-shaped walls in an overlapping field (*figure 75*). Another set of sketches displays the initial square, a shift in one direction to create the long rectangle, and then a shift in a perpendicular direction, which opens the plan for entry and promenade, delineated by a twisted, curvilinear line that runs through the plan. This last sketch is closest to the final plan and reveals, along with the finished product, similarities to the plan of the Basilica that are too numerous and exact to pass over (see *figure 60*).

Basically the Basilica plan displaces one square from an initial square to the point of rest, where the two are inscribed in a golden rectangle (*figure 76*). The internal sides of these squares fall on the structural and spatial divisions of the vaults of the building's main body. The Danteum is composed of the same shifting squares (*figure 77*), but in addi-

79

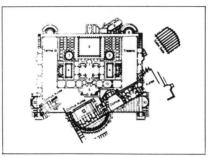

72 Domus Aurea, Rome. Plan included on the Danteum site plan.

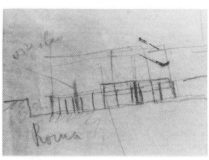

73 Danteum, Scheme *A*. Detail showing a section. On the drawing are written the words *Roma* and *Virgil*.

74 Terragni, Sketch #0250, possibly for the Danteum.

75 Terragni, Unnumbered sketch showing overlapping squares.

tion to the initial golden rectangle, a larger rectangle is created through the transverse displacement of the shifted squares (*figure 78*). Terragni does *not* seem preoccupied with the simplicity of the Basilica plan in terms of the correspondence of the geometric figure to actual forms in space; he simply allows one square to be expressed in the dimension of the front wall of the courtyard alone.

Another source for this composition is the plan of Le Corbusier's Villa Stein at Garches (1927), an important inspiration to Terragni in the thirties. While this source is conjecture on my part, it seems likely in view of Terragni's preoccupation with abstract formal qualities in other architectures. The plan of the Villa at Garches is composed of a geometric pattern that can be broken down easily into a pair of overlapping squares in the manner of the Basilica of Maxentius and the Danteum (*figure 79*). In addition, the plan of the Villa at Garches has the ratio of the golden section and a narrow strip, similar to the Danteum plan, with a layer of space in front and rear. In other words, if we remove either the front or rear strip of space, we have a golden-section rectangle just like the Danteum. While it is unlikely that Le Corbusier conceived his house for Leo Stein in the same terms that Terragni conceived the Danteum, it is likely that Terragni indeed did view the Corbusian prototype in the manner just described.

Returning to the Basilica of Maxentius, we find that all the major spaces of this "illustratious work," as Terragni called it, are either squares or golden sections (*figure 80*). The same is true for the Danteum (*figure 81*) insofar as those spaces are perceptible, even as figures to be read in the plan alone. The resulting outside figure of the Danteum, before the lateral displacement, is a golden rectangle like the Basilica, and the wider figure obtained after displacement is equivalent to the proportion of the Basilica when the portico on the long facade is included (*figures 82 and 83*). The peripheries of both buildings are similar. Narrow layers of space at the ends of each composition further link the buildings: they are the apsidal zone and the portico on the short end of the Basilica, and the stairway to the Paradise and the transition from the Inferno to Purgatory in the Danteum.

Finally, the retaining wall of the Basilica that was imitated in the Palazzo Littorio Solution *A* was imitated in the Danteum, maintaining the symmetry across the Via dell'Impero. In the Danteum the wall became no more than a freestanding facade. It was to be "similar to the

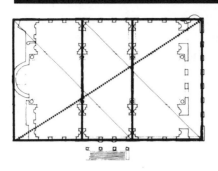

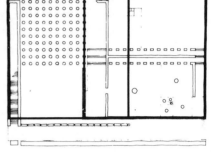

82 76 Basilica of Maxentius. Plan. Analysis of the squares and golden section created by the slipping of the initial squares.

77 Danteum. Initial generating squares, slipped in one direction to form the primary golden section.

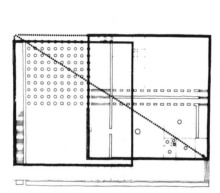

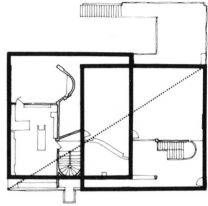

78 Danteum. Squares slipped in the transverse direction to form the overall composition.

79 Le Corbusier, Villa Stein at Garches, 1927. Plan. The overall golden section and squares of this plan may be read as a two-directional slippage of squares.

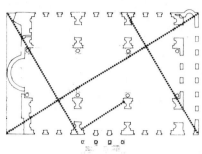

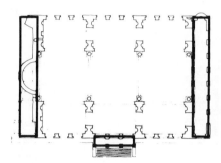

80 Basilica of Maxentius. Decomposition of the golden rectangle.

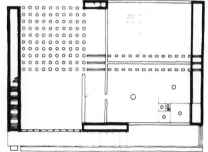

81 Danteum. Decomposition of the golden rectangle.

82 Basilica of Maxentius. End zones in the composition.

83 Danteum. End zones in the composition.

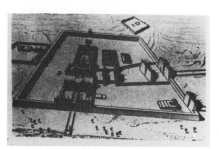

84 The Temple Complex at Karnak, Egypt. Perspective included on the Danteum site plan. The encircling walls dominate.

86 The Palace at Sargon, Persia. Perspective included on the Danteum site plan. The platforms dominate.

85 Serlio, Hypostyle hall, called "Senate House." Plan.

87 Terragni, Church painting. Oil on canvas.

Pelasgic walls that are so well preserved on the Greek peninsula and in the Aegean Islands," and would reflect "the universality of the Roman Empire polemically expounded in *De Monarchia* and the *Convivio* [Dante's earlier works] and later exalted in the marvelous tercets of the 'Poem.'" [2]

In addition to the aforementioned sources for the composition of the building plan, there are a number of "found objects" collaged into the project and drawings in a manner similar to the site plan for the Palazzo Littorio Solution *A*. The most obvious of these are the two images pasted onto the site plan of the Danteum. One is the Karnak Temple complex in Egypt (*figure 84*). The caption reads, "Rigid rectilinear geometry. The Monumental partitions determine the intellectual rhythm." Terragni also borrowed the Egyptian hypostyle hall for the portico of the Danteum. The hypostyle hall has another probable source in *Serlio,* a reference book well known to Italian architects of Terragni's generation (*figure 85*). The plan is Serlio's idea of an ancient Greek "Council Hall," which he calls "the creation of the first intentions of good architecture." [3]

The frontal wall of the typical Egyptian temple is similar enough to the Pelasgic walls of the ancient Aegean for Terragni to believe he had a double source in such a motif. One may suggest as well that Terragni's facade be read as the facade of a medieval church; i.e., a portal as well as a backdrop for some modern version of a medieval morality play to be performed in front of Dante's temple.

If we follow the idea of multiple sources (similar to multiple readings or intentions), we can construct Terragni's concept of historical relevance. To begin with, he subsumed the Assyrians, Egyptians, Greeks, and Romans under one category of ancient architecture. Part of this tendency may be attributed to Terragni's desire to identify with architectures and peoples who once lived under the Pax Romana; part may be his desire to find some common theoretical ground for *all* architectures.

Thus Terragni included an illustration of the Palace of Sargon in Persia (8 B.C.) (*figure 86*) along with the Egyptian temples. The caption reads, "Notice how the hierarchic distinctions of the various parts of the palace are [made] in the horizontal rather than in the vertical plane." The two references support each other as sources for all compositional elements, the former for *walls,* the latter for *floors.* Each example possesses the simplest and most elemental version of an architectonic organization, like the Danteum. The hypostyle hall also resembles the mosques of Constantinople, as Rocchi has noticed. [4] The columns themselves, however, seem to derive from a source closer to home: the medieval church of S. Abbondio in Como, beloved by Terragni. He painted at least two oils of this church, a facade and an interior of the five-aisled basilica that closely resembles his rendering of the columns of the Danteum (*figure 87*).

The glass columns of the Paradise (*plate 15*), however, certainly derive from Bertoia's painting in Parma, the *Sala del Bacio* (1566–1577) (*figure 88*). The painting displays crystal columns supporting gilt entablatures and beams, partially open to the sky, with an open landscape background, peopled with dancing, embracing, and kissing figures. Sydney Freedberg describes this painting as possessing a "disarming cavalier illogic ... fragile and exquisite in form, [the figures] seem creatures resurrected from some Tanagrene antiquity, but they are moved by a spirit that is bizarre as well as playful." [5] Similar adjectives are appropriate for what appears to be Terragni's design for the Paradise, with columns rendered concrete and nonexistent at the same time. The participants of Terragni's Paradise, were they in fact imagined like those of the *Sala del Bacio,* would have brought a fascinating twist to Dante's concept of heaven. The question of whether Terragni saw the painting in situ is still unanswered. It is in the Palazzo Ducale in Parma, which was an army headquarters in the late twenties, when Terragni performed his first military service; he was stationed in Piacenza and Cremona, not far from Parma. It is possible that he did indeed see the fresco.

A final piece of architectural collage is the freestanding screen at the rear facade of the entry court (*figure 89*). Terragni makes no reference to it in the *Relazione;* it appears in only two of the final drawings and does not appear on the model. The screen, which resembles any number of frame constructions of the fascist period in Italy, displays montaged photographs of sculpture, some of which originated in Greek Sicily (*figure 90*). (Among the sculptures are Europa and Hercules from Selinus, Sicily.) While the specific references of the photos are unclear, the screen serves as a modern version of a temple-front, complete with

86

88 Il Bertoia, *Sala del Bacio*, Ducal Palace, Parma,
1566–1577. Fresco.

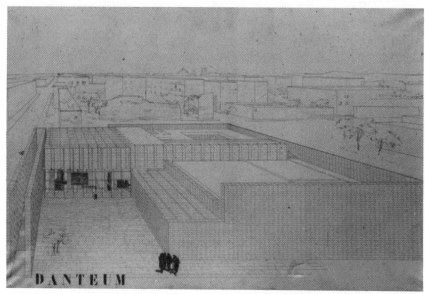

88

89 Danteum. Aerial perspective of court.

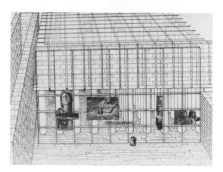

90 Danteum. Detail of court perspective. A "modern" portico with a new way to display "pediment" sculpture.

pedimental sculptures. In what is otherwise a wall architecture, the screen at first appears foreign to the design. It may have been drawn by Marcello Nizzoli, who helped in presentation, but the concept was clearly Terragni's. [6] This secondary facade contains nine bays and ten "columns," reminiscent of ancient Greek ten-column temples. The proportions of the screen and of the facade behind, which Terragni called a "portico," are almost exactly those of the Parthenon. At the very least, Terragni was thinking of modern equivalents for historical forms and elements, indicated by his constant written allusions and design intentions.

The screen serves as the structural frame, and in this way characterizes Italian rationalism. For Terragni and the rationalists, the frame was quite different in concept from the frame of Le Corbusier, Mies, or other proponents of "frame" architecture. As Colin Rowe has shown, the frame was of particular iconic and polemical importance to the International Style. [7] It represented the concept of a building method that was believed to bring both quality in design and the amelioration of social ills. As Rowe explains, "For the International Style ... the frame is a guarantee of authenticity.... " [8] More specifically, to Le Corbusier the frame is the image of a dialogue between a construction system and a layered spatial system. For Mies it is the grid of a universal wrapper, a kind of string shopping bag that defines universal space without literally enclosing it. These attitudes are manifested by the normal location of the frame in each architect's work. In Le Corbusier's buildings the frame is usually remotely within the skin; for Mies it is normally coincident with the skin. For Terragni, however, the frame is often *outside* the skin, and the skin is itself expressed as a plane behind. The frame is more rhetorical than literal; it is a decorative element that recalls past architectures, a sign of entry, a porch.

The structural subversion makes manifest the rhetoric, and the historical reference is aimed directly at quattrocento and cinquecento architecture, periods when the development of the frame as an ordering device for the facade reached a peak in the work of Alberti, Sangallo, Giulio Romano, and most notably, Vignola (*figure 91*). Terragni was partial to this period (see Luigi Zuccoli's memories in Zevi, *Omàggio a Terragni*), and his tendency to equate geometric order with rational process is expressed in the use of the frame as an abstract ordering

91 Vignola, Palazzo Farnese, Caprarola. Facade.

device, stripped of *most* of its structural characteristics. It is important to distinguish Terragni's expropriation and abstraction of the frame from the arches and columns of the Piacentiniani, which were simply "servile imitation" (Zuccoli's paraphrase of Terragni's term).

Terragni's frame, then, became a modern construction motif justified by its modernity. Thus the screen as the portico to the Danteum has a hyperbolic significance. While the Danteum contains only this single frame in the vertical plane, another frame appears in the covering of the ultimate space of the building, the Paradise, where it frames the view to the heavens, as the skylights frame the view in the Purgatory. [9] It is an architectural motif in the process of *becoming,* and its appearance is almost ironic, as if Terragni were making the statement that he need not rely on *any* palpable architectonic motif but on the relationships of pure geometry alone. Beyond the anti-Piacentini (or better, anti-Ojetti) statement of inverting the column-wall formula, there lurks an antimodern (or International Style) statement. This lies in the total return to traditional structure (column-entablature and bearing wall), avoiding the stark white planes of the "style."

In its ironic denial of aspects of the rationalist and monumentalist mainstreams, this most personal of Terragni's buildings becomes exactly what he demanded of it: a dematerialized spiritual fact. And while the Danteum may be seen as a typical fascist design object, intended as a preparation for political-spiritual experience, an affirmation of faith in the fascist ideology, and a warning to those who would forsake Italian national necessities for individual goals, it is also a building that breaks implicit rules of the modern movement.

Like Le Corbusier, Terragni eludes attempts to categorize his architecture. After initially embracing the modern movement precepts, he wrote in 1931:

> We use rationalism to arrive at Architecture, not architecture to arrive at rationalism ... there is the serene and clear rationalism, almost Mediterranean, of certain Hellenic buildings, and there is the barbaric rationalism of certain typical Nordic architects; there is the rationalism that gives rise to houses and villas made for a life under the sun, amidst trees and flowers, facing the water; and there is the rationalism that gives life to the inhumane visions of squalor and nightmares. [10]

1. *Relazione,* para. 3.

2. *Ibid.,* para. 13.

3. See George Hersey, *Pythagorean Palaces, Magic and Architecture in the Italian Renaissance* (Ithaca: Cornell University Press, 1976).

4. In *L'Architettura* 163.

5. See Sydney Freedberg, *Painting in Italy 1500–1600,* Pelican History of Art (Baltimore: Penguin Books, 1970), 401. For this discovery I am indebted to Judith de Maio.

6. In an interview with the author, Luigi Zuccoli said he believed the screen to have been drawn by Nizzoli.

7. See Colin Rowe, "Chicago Frame," *Architectural Review* (Nov. 1956), reprinted in Colin Rowe, *The Mathematics of the Ideal Villa and Other Essays* (Cambridge: MIT Press, 1976).

8. *Ibid.*

9. The extant text of the *Relazione* trails off with the phrase "framed by geometry" in the description of the space of Purgatory.

10. From Mantero, *Giuseppe Terragni,* 103–104.

Where we do not reflect on Myth but truly live in it, there is no cleft between the actual reality of perception and the world of mythical fantasy.

Ernst Cassirer, The Philosophy of Symbolic Forms

THE
RELAZIONE

WE MAY APPROACH TERRAGNI'S REPORT IN TERMS of its sources in Dante as we have approached the Danteum in terms of its sources. I have therefore reprinted here the text of the *Relazione* with excerpts from Dante's *Divine Comedy, Vita Nuova, De Monarchia, Convivio,* and *Epistle to Can Grande della Scala.* [1] The text of the *Relazione* begins on page two of the extant typescript.

1 ... the series of the Imperial Fora of Trajan, Augustus, Nerva, and Vespasian, with a northwest, southeast direction. The Via dell'Impero is inserted in the space determined by the two groupings of buildings that lie mainly on the second (southwest) side of the street. The ruins that flank the Via dell'Impero are disposed at a slight angle to the street, slightly inclined to face the Colosseum itself.

96

I will now in the capacity of commentator essay a few words by way of introduction to the work which is offered for your acceptance. [*Epistle to Can Grande,* para. 4]

2 The Area established by the technical office of the government for the construction of the Danteum is of a nongeometric shape, the edge of which describes an irregular polygon. Our first task was to study the possibility of inserting a geometrically *regular* plan-form into such an accidental shape.

3 The round form was discarded because the area it encloses is too modest for what was needed, but also because of the immediacy of potential conflict with the perfect and imposing ellipse of the Colosseum. It was necessary to turn our attention to a rectangle in order to arrive at the particular one that would imprint, through the happy relation of its two dimensions, that value of "absolute" geometric beauty onto the entire structure of

All things have order among themselves, and this is the form that makes the universe like God. Herein the high creatures behold the imprint of the Eternal Worth, which is the end wherefor the aforesaid ordinance is made. [*Paradise* I, 103–108]

the monument; this being the tendency of the exemplary architectures of the great historical epochs.

4 Meanwhile it was impossible to escape our preoccupation as designers with the problems of grafting onto geometric schemes for the monument — from the very beginning — meanings, myths, and commonly held symbols as a spiritual synthesis. And in the case of Dante's works these are evidently *numerical* meanings.

5 The connection between the plastic-architectonic expression and the abstraction and symbolism of the theme of the building (a connection that could cast doubt on the relevance and spontaneity of the results) was only possible at the *origin* of those two discrete spiritual facts: building and poem. Architectural monument and literary work can adhere to a *singular* scheme without losing, in this union, any of each work's essential qualities only if both possess a structure and a harmonic rule that can allow them to confront each other, so that they may then be read in a geometric or mathematical relation of parallelism or subordination. In our case the architecture could adhere to the literary work only through

Different virtues must needs be fruits of formal principles, the which, save only one, would be destroyed, according to your reckoning.
[*Paradise* II, 70–72]

Now of things which exist, some are such as to have absolute being in themselves; while others are such as to have their being dependent upon something else, by virtue of a certain relation, as being in existence at the same time, or having respect to some other thing, as in the case of correlatives, such as father and son, master and servant, double and half, the whole and part, and other similar things, in so far as they are related.
[*Epistle to Can Grande*, para. 5]

an examination of the admirable structure of the Divine Poem, itself faithful to a criterion of division and interpretation through certain symbolic numbers: 1, 3, 7, 10 and their combinations, which happily can be synthesized into *one* and *three* (unity and trinity).

6 Now, there is only one rectangle that clearly expresses the harmonic law of unity in trinity, and this is the rectangle known historically as the "golden"; the rectangle, that is, whose sides are in the golden ratio (the short side is to the long side as the long side is to the sum of the two sides). *One* is the rectangle, *three* are the segments that determine the golden ratio. And furthermore, such a rectangle is capable of being decomposed into a square of a side equal to the short side and another golden rectangle of sides equal, respectively, to the short side and the difference between the two sides of the original rectangle. In its turn, such a smaller golden rectangle may be decomposed into a square and a golden rectangle, and thus it goes — through these possible decompositions is manifested the concept of the infinite — because such decompositions are in fact infinite.

7 The golden-section rectangle is

Foolish is he who hopes that our reason may compass the infinite course taken by One Substance in Three Persons.
[*Purgatory* III, 34–36]

The number three is the root of nine, because, independent of any other number, multiplied by itself alone, it makes nine ... if three is the sole factor of nine, and the sole factor of miracles is three, that is, Father, Son, and Holy Ghost, who are three and one....
[*Vita Nuova* XXIX, 20–29]

98

Plate 1 Danteum. View to Colosseum. Watercolor panel, foldout.

Plate 2 Danteum. Front view. Watercolor panel,
foldout.

one of the plan-forms frequently adopted by the ancient Assyrians, Egyptians, Greeks, and Romans. These peoples have left behind typical examples of rectangular plan temples in which the golden rectangle is used; and most often composed with numerical relationships as well. The most evident example lies in the Via dell'Impero in the form of the Basilica of Maxentius, whose plan is a golden rectangle.

8 The plan thus adopted for the Danteum is the rectangle similar to that of the Basilica of Maxentius and dimensionally directly derived from that illustratious Roman construct. The long side of the Danteum is equal to the short side of the Basilica, while the short side is consequently equal to the difference between the two sides of the Basilica. Once the form, dimension, and orientation of the building are determined in this way, it is then necessary to proceed in such a way that would respect the harmonic law imposed by the golden rectangle. Of particular importance in the composition of the fundamental elements of the work is also the rule and the relationship established by the numbers 1 and 3; 1, 3 and 7; 1, 3, 7, and 10; numerical law that is

And had it not been that on that dike the slope was shorter than on the other, I know not about him, but I should have been quite vanquished. But because all Malebolge inclines toward the mouth of the nethermost well, the site of each valley is such that one side is higher and the other lower.
[*Inferno* XXIV, 34–42]

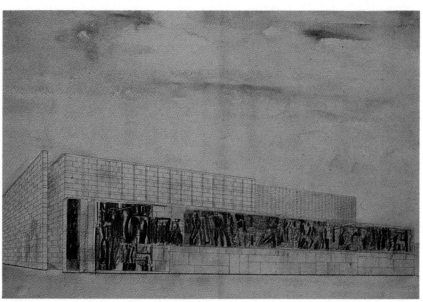

Plate 3 Danteum. Detail of front perspective, with Sironi reliefs photographed and pasted onto the drawing.

found in the *Divine Comedy*. To superimpose two rules, one geometric, the other numerical, is to achieve equilibrium and logic in the selection of dimensions, spaces, heights, and thicknesses for the purpose of establishing a plastic fact of absolute values, spiritually chained to Dantesque compositional criteria. This also serves to obtain a higher value, at the same time avoiding the imminent danger of falling into rhetoricism, into symbolism, or into convention. If the Dantesque Inferno, for instance, were to be plastically delineated by a series of diminishing rings in the form of a funnel, ending in the vertex of the Devil, with the intervals, jumps, bridges, rivers, etc., so admirably described by the Divine Poet, this would almost certainly *not* create an exciting effect because the presentation would be too literal a version of Dante's description.

9 It is necessary, therefore, that the plastic means be itself an expression of absolute geometric beauty. The spiritual reference and direct dependence upon the first canto of the Poem must be expressed in unmistakable signs by an atmosphere that influences the visitor and appears physically to weigh upon his mortal person, so

Ah, how hard it is to tell what that wood was, wild, rugged, harsh; the very thought of it renews the fear! It is so bitter that death is hardly more so. But, to treat of the good that I found in it, I will tell of the other things I saw there.
[*Inferno* I, 4–9]

DANTEUM VISTA DALLA TORRE

Plate 4 Danteum. Perspective.

that he is moved to experience the "trip" as Dante did. He must be touched by the contemplation of this adventure and of the pains of the sinners whom Dante met throughout his sad pilgrimage. Such a state of mind is difficult enough to relate with the aid of words and poetic imagination, or with the plastic means of proportions and volumes of architecture. But the difficulty is then enlarged by the danger of obtaining results that are too remote from what is needed. Thus we have reexamined the problem with our minds liberated from the preoccupation of literally following the text of the Magnificent Account. Instead, we place our attention on a problem that is closer to our sensibilities and our preparation as architects; which is to imagine and translate into *stone* an architectural organism that, through the balanced proportion of its walls, ramps, stairs, ceilings, the play of its ever-changing light from the sun above, can give to he who traverses its internal spaces the sensation of contemplative isolation, of removal from the external world, which is so often permeated by the noises of life and feverish anxiety of movement and traffic.

I began, "Poet, you who guide me, consider if my strength is sufficient, before you trust me to the deep way."
[*Inferno* II, 10–12]

Ah, justice of God! who crams together so many new travails and penalties as I saw? And why does our guilt so waste us? As does the wave, there over Charybdis, breaking itself against the wave it meets, so must the folk here dance their round.
[*Inferno* VII, 19–24]

Every substantial form that is both distinct from matter and united with it, holds within itself a specific virtue, which is not perceived except through operation nor ever shows itself save by its effect, as life in a plant by the green leaves.
[*Purgatory* XVIII, 49–54]

Neither Creator nor creature, my son, was ever without love, either natural or of the mind, and this you know. The natural is always without error; but the other may err either through an evil object, or through too much or too little vigor.
[*Purgatory* XVII, 91–96]

10 Three rectangular spaces

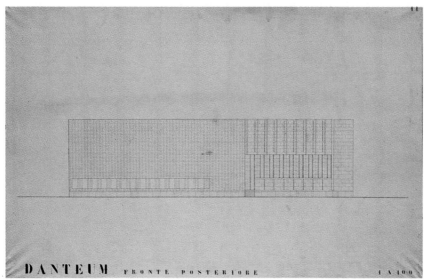

Plate 5 Danteum. Rear facade.

declare, in a clear manner, the theme of the rectangle already taken in relation to and derived from the golden rectangle of the Basilica of Maxentius. There remains a fourth space defined by the binding walls of the building and, since it is excluded from the scheme of the *three* fundamental spaces of the philosophical structure of the Poem, it is also excluded from the architectural organism, thereby determining a *closed court,* comparable to the *orto concluso* [closed garden] of the typical Latin house or the atrium, open to the sky, of the Etruscan house. This symbolism can add meaning to this space "intentionally wasted" from the point of view of building economy, and we can thus speak of a reference to the life of Dante up to his thirty-fifth year of age, a life of transgression into error and sin, and therefore "lost" in the moral and philosophical balance, when the life of the poet is taken as an example of the reformation and salvation of a corrupt and sinful mankind. The important thing to note here is that the meaning, or reading, of the symbol is not so important so as to obscure the effective plastic necessity and harmony of the composition. Avoidance of this necessity would create a *hole* in the

I passed easily through heats and frosts, content in contemplative thoughts.
[*Paradise* XXI, 116–117]

Midway in the journey of our life I found myself in a dark wood, for the straight way was lost.
[*Inferno* I, 3]

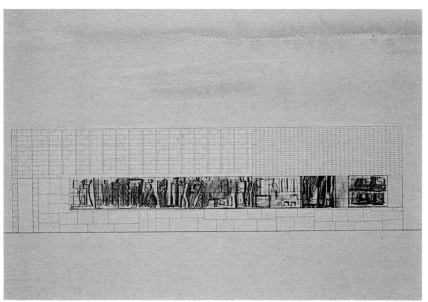

Plate 6 Danteum. Facade with Sironi reliefs.

architectonic structure. Thus we can say the same of all the connections found in the building that have the value of analogue or reference to conditions beyond having solved the problems of equilibrium and architectonic harmony. Here, in fact, is the "forest" of 100 marble columns in a square of twenty meters on a side, each of which supports an element of the floor above, situated eight meters above the plane of the court. This architectonic motif, of great plastic effect, is first of all the entry portico to the rooms of the Danteum. The image of the Dantesque forest can be suggested by contiguity with the continuous open space of the court (the life of Dante before his subterranean trip) and the necessity for the visitor to traverse such a space as a prelude to the rooms dedicated to the three *cantiche* of the *Comedy*. The entrance to the building, then, situated parallel to and behind the facade, and between two high walls of marble, further restated by another long wall parallel to the front, can also correspond to another Dantesque "justification": *"non so ben come v'entrai"* [I do not know how I entered]. This securely establishes the character of pilgrimage that visitors must make, lining

Through me you enter the Woeful City, through me you enter Eternal Grief.
[*Inferno* III, 1–2]

Plate 7 Danteum. Detail of Sironi reliefs.

processionally in single file, and guided only by the intense sunlight that will be reflected on the square space of the court.

Always before him stands a crowd of them; they go, each in his turn, to the judgment....
[*Inferno* V, 13–14]

11 From the golden rectangle that coincides with the generating plan of the building are developed the fundamental lines, such as the square constructed from the minor side, the most easily perceived characteristic of the work. The square is revealed in the plan at level 1.60m and in the approach to the study rooms of the ground floor. The same scheme is created on the opposite side, where the frontal wall is displaced in front of and parallel to the major side of the golden rectangle, thereby creating another pure square. This displacement of walls also creates the entry passage. Hence, the long flight of stairs of seven landings is the result of the difference between the golden rectangle of the generating plan and the square of the body of the building proper at the ground plane. It then follows that the mathematical and geometric correspondences can be traced in turn for the most important divisions of the rooms of the building — deriving the workings of the plan from the decomposition of the golden rectangle. To the functional plan scheme of a

Up by the three steps, with my good will, my leader drew me.
[*Purgatory* IX, 106–107]

In like manner the form of the part is determined by that of the whole work. For if the form of the treatise as a whole is threefold, in this part it is twofold only, the division being that of the cantica and of the cantos.
[*Epistle to Can Grande,* para. 12]

Plate 8 Danteum. View through the internal
"street" toward the Colosseum.

111

cruciform shape that determines the partitioning into *one* (open court) and *three* (the large temple-like rooms dedicated to the three *cantiche* — Inferno, Purgatory, Paradise) is overlaid a scheme of vertical measure (the three rooms are situated at three levels respectively at 2.70m, 5.40m, and 8.10m dimensions, which are all multiples of three).

12 These two fundamental schemes are intersected by a third scheme formed by the "longitudinal spine" that is constituted of three walls (alternatingly solid and perforated) defining, at the top of the building, the room dedicated to the Imperial concept of Dante. This room of fundamental spiritual importance comes to represent the germ of the architectural whole as the conclusion of the experience of the spaces traversed — from the Inferno, to the Purgatory, to the Paradise. It can therefore be interpreted as the central nave of a temple, dominating and giving light to the minor spaces. The reference to the theme is clear:

13 The universal Roman Empire that was envisaged and forecast by Dante as the ultimate purpose and the only remedy for saving

And the form is twofold — the form of the treatise and the form of the treatment. The form of the treatise is threefold, according to the threefold division. The first division is that whereby the whole work is divided into three cantiche; the second, whereby each cantica is divided into cantos; and the third, whereby each canto is divided into rhymed lines.
[*Epistle to Can Grande,* para. 9]

The glory of the All-Mover penetrates through the universe and reglows in one part more, and in another less. I have been in the heaven that most receives of His light, and have seen things which whoso descends from up there has neither the knowledge nor the power to relate, because, as it draws near to its desire, our intellect enters so deep that memory cannot go back upon the track.
[*Paradise* I, 1–3]

And you shall be with me forever a citizen of that Rome whereof Christ is Roman. Therefore, for profit of the world that lives ill,

112

Plate 9 Danteum. Court perspective.

humanity and the Church from disorder and corruption. The allusions, references, and citations can
be seen most often in the *Divine
Comedy* and in the transitions
between Inferno, Purgatory, and
Paradise. The parts dedicated to
this vision and prophecy of the
Empire progress throughout the
Poem and therefore will progress
throughout the spaces that seek to
exalt the Poem. It is necessary
here to remember which element
in the architectonic structure of
the Danteum is a strict analogy to
the room dedicated to the Empire:
it is the monumental wall that is
disposed parallel to the front and
displays a long frieze of relief
sculptures to the Via dell'Impero.
It is thus similar to the Pelasgic
walls that are so well preserved on
the Greek peninsula and on the
Aegean Islands. This wall, which
hides the building, creates an
internal street of slight incline that
leads to entry and leaves the view
to the Colosseum visually free for
the visitor who approaches from
Piazza Venezia. But above all, this
wall recalls the character of the fa-
cing Basilica of Maxentius, thus
expressing and explaining the
lesson of the universality of the
Roman Empire that Dante polemically expounded in *De Monarchia*
and the *Convivio* and later exalted

hold your eyes now on the chariot,
and what you see, mind that you
write it when you have returned
yonder.
[*Purgatory* XXXII, 100–105]

I, therefore, who was now turned
to the seashore where the water of
Tiber grows salt, was kindly gath-
ered in by him. To that river-
mouth he has now set his wings,
for there the souls are always
gathering that sink not down to
Acheron.
[*Purgatory* II, 100–106]

There is a place in Hell called
Malebolge, all of stone which is
the color of iron, like the wall that
goes round it.
[*Inferno* XVIII, 1–3]

Not yet had we moved our feet on
it when I perceived that the encircling band (which, being vertical,
lacked means of ascent) was of
pure white marble, and was
adorned with such carvings that
not only Polycletus but Nature
herself would there be put to

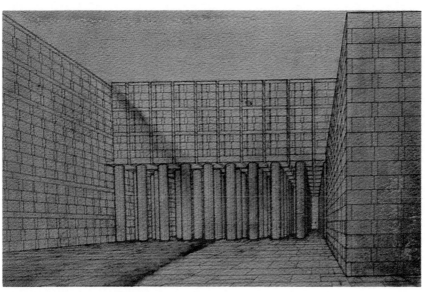

Plate 10 Danteum. Court detail. Dante's life
before his "allegorical trip."

in the marvelous tercets of the Poem. In this way the wall becomes an immense blackboard, a monumental table filled with 100 marble blocks (equivalent to the cantos of the *Comedy*), each in size proportional to its place in the scheme of its canto. They therefore vary in size, and this explains the free composition, the model for which is found in Homeric Greece. The tercets or the verses containing the allusions, the references, and the allegory of the Empire will be incised on the facade within the blocks corresponding to the canto from which each is derived. The monolithic block at the head of the sequence, on the Piazza Venezia side, is the *greyhound*.

14 In this way it will be documented that the providential coincidence of choosing the zone of the Via dell'Impero for a monument to Dante could not but create a great spiritual response and a very *certain* prediction.

15 The moral system of the Inferno is traced with fundamental lines in the lesson given to Dante by Virgil in Canto XI (the structure of Hell). This, however, is the Aristotelian concept that for Dante is a pagan concept of

shame.
[*Purgatory* X, 28–33]

Accursed be you, ancient wolf, who have more prey than all the other beasts, because of your hunger endlessly deep! O heaven, in whose revolution it seems conditions here below are thought to be changed, when will he come through whom she shall depart?
[*Purgatory* XX, 10–15]

Many are the beasts with which she mates, and there will yet be more, until the Hound shall come who will deal her a painful death.
[*Inferno* I, 100–103]

"Philosophy, for one who understands it," he said to me, "points out, not in one place alone, how

DANTEUM INFERNO

Plate 11 Danteum. Room of the Inferno. Scant
light, oppressive atmosphere.

117

reason; this moral topography is valid up to the point where it must then be sustained by the cardinal and theological virtues. It then follows that the worst sins or capital vices and hence bad dispositions that contrast to the three theological and the four cardinal virtues are considered here as the real major decompositions of the moral structure of the Inferno and Purgatory — thus they may be glimpsed in the "architecture" of the Poem. And the second of Virgil's lessons on the organization of Purgatory (Canto XVII) is the more exact classification of faults already described in Canto XI of the Inferno. The two cantos together form the correct response between the *seven* frames of Purgatory and the *nine* rings of the Inferno. This is not a paradoxical affirmation because in the Inferno one is being punished for faults provoked by the seven sins and in Purgatory only for a moral blot; it is logical that, at first, Dante would have followed a more analytical classification, extending it to consider some finer-grained subdivisions (nine versus seven). These premises are necessary to give an exhaustive explanation to the composition of the two rooms of the Inferno and Purgatory as they are represented in the

Nature takes her course from divine Intellect and from Its art; and if you note well your *Physics,* you will find, after not many pages, that your art, as far as it can, follows her, as the pupil does his master; so that your art is as it were grandchild of God."
[*Inferno* XI, 97–104]

"My son, within these rocks," he then began, "are three lesser circles, one below another, like those you are leaving.
"All are full of accursed spirits; but in order that hereafter the sight alone may suffice you, hear how and why they are impounded."
[*Inferno* XI, 16–18]

While it is directed on the Primal Good, and on secondary goods observes right measure, it cannot be the cause of sinful pleasure. But when it is turned awry to evil, or speeds to good with more zeal, or with less, than it ought, against the Creator works His creature. Hence you can comprehend that love must needs be the seed in you of every virtue and of every action deserving punishment.
[*Purgatory* XVII, 97–105]

118

Plate 12 Danteum. Detail of Inferno columns.

drawings of the Danteum. We have already seen how the plan of each room coincides with a golden-section rectangle that is one quarter of the total area of the larger golden rectangle that determines the entire composition.

16 The rule of unity and trinity is therefore contained in the rectangle itself as it is rigorously respected in the "symmetrical" division of the Poem: three *cantiche* of thirty-three cantos each plus a *canto* of introduction. The 100 cantos that result are equal to the *square* of *ten,* symbol of perfection (3 X 3 + 1). The same rhythm that is the basis for the tercet is re-taken as an analogy in the subdivision of the marble coursing of the building: three courses of equal height, one string course assigned to correspond to a level of each of the three rooms, for which floor and ceiling of four rooms (the terrestrial life of Dante, the Inferno, Purgatory, Paradise) are plotted on the facade by seven bands that interrupt the stone ashlar disposed at intervals of three.

All the first circle is for the violent: but because violence is done to three persons, it is divided and constructed in three rings. To God, to one's self, and to one's neighbor may violence be done: I say to them and to their things, as I shall make plain to you. [*Inferno* XI, 28–32]

17 Seven are the mortal sins, seven the theological and cardinal virtues (3 + 4), seven the days taken by Dante in the allegorical trip begun

Plate 13 Danteum. Room of the Purgatory.
Aspiration framed by geometry.

on the seventh of April in 1300 (Holy Thursday in the Jubilee year).

18 The adherence of the architectural and the compositional artifact to the numerical rule of symmetry and retracing the subdivisions of the walls and the fundamental dimensions of the rooms, e.g., the floor-to-ceiling height of 8.10 meters (81 decimeters, 3 X 3 X 3 X 3 decimeters), are not sufficient to explain the structure of the rooms themselves. It is necessary to also refer to a more general problem, taking into account two limits:

1) Research into *essentials,* in an interpretation of the Poem, involving three modes of discourse: the *literal,* the *allegorical,* and the *anagogical.*

2) The character of an architecture and the definition of a type for a monumental building that must avail itself of two or more already historically fixed types in the form of Temple, Museum, Tomb, Palace, and Theater.

19 The *literal* sense is the description of the extraterrestrial trip that forms part of the cycle of medieval poetry on the destiny of man (the voyage of St. Paul, the purgatory of St. Patrick, etc.) and joins

... the ladies began, alternating, now three, now four....
[*Purgatory* XXXIII, 1–2]

"Son, what are you gazing at up there?" And I to him, "At those three torches with which the pole here is all aflame." And he to me, "The four bright stars you saw this morning are low on the other side, and these are risen where those were."
[*Purgatory* VIII, 86–93]

For the elucidation, therefore, of what we have to say, it must be understood that the meaning of this work is not of one kind only; rather the work may be described as "polysemous," that is, having several meanings; for the first meaning is that which is conveyed by the letter, and the next is that which is conveyed by what the letter signifies; the former of which is called literal, while the latter is called allegorical, or mystical.
[*Epistle to Can Grande,* para. 7]

Now this man, who from the lowest pit of the universe even to here has seen one by one the spiritual lives, implores thee of thy grace for power such that he may be able with his eyes to rise still

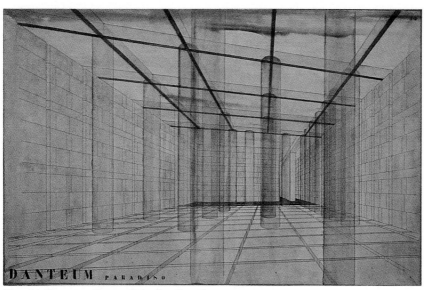

Plate 14 Danteum. Room of the Paradise. A
room floating above the everyday world.

perfection, in the artistic sense, with higher Christian goals. The *allegorical* is the amelioration of Dante (sinful humanity) through consideration of sin (Inferno), in the expiation of penitence (Purgatory), and into Grace (Paradise). The *anagogical* sense is the vision of eternal happiness for humanity (recaptured in the person of Dante) and obtained with the reconstruction of the Roman Empire with its center in Rome, for worldy prosperity, and restoration of the Church — now liberated from the temporal power that pollutes it — for spiritual happiness, with its center also in Rome.

20 The research into *essentials* in these three areas brings us to consider the last eminent didactic quality of the building; this would be valued as the "pretext" of the work if this marvelous epoch in which we live were not such a limpid confirmation of Dante's "dowry" of prophecy.

21 To exalt the *Divine Comedy* with an architectural monument is thus a living work and not a labor of erudition nor the fantasy of a theatrical producer.

22 Therefore it is not a museum, not a palace, not a theater, but a

higher toward the last salvation. [*Paradise* XXXIII, 22–27]

The aim of the whole and of the part might be manifold; as, for instance, immediate and remote. But leaving aside any minute examination of this question, it may be stated briefly that the aim of the whole and of the part is to remove those living in this life from a state of misery, and to bring them to a state of happiness. [*Epistle to Can Grande,* para. 15]

... the supreme pontiff, to lead the human race, in accordance with things revealed, to eternal life; and the emperor, to direct the human race to temporal felicity in accordance with the teachings of philosophy.... Let Caesar, therefore, observe that reverence to Peter which a first-born son should observe to a father.... [*De Monarchia* III, xvi]

There storied was the high glory of the Roman prince whose worth moved Gregory to his great victory: I mean the Emperor Trajan. And a poor widow was at his bridle in attitude of weeping and of grief. Round about him appeared a trampling and throng of horsemen, and above them the ea-

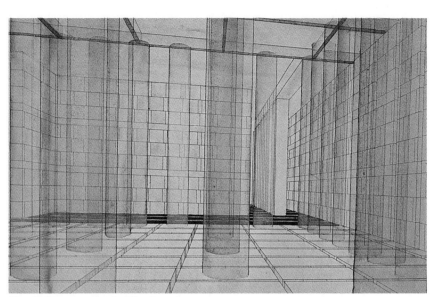

Plate 15 Danteum. Detail of Paradise columns.

Temple that we wish to construct.

23 A tripartite Temple of rooms disposed at different levels establishes an ascending route. Constructed in different ways, these rooms are integrated to gradually prepare the visitor for a sublimation of matter and light. The room of the Inferno, heavy and discreetly lighted by slits in the ceiling, seeks to establish by first contact with the visitor the spiritual atmosphere of astonishment through its peculiar and suggestive arrangement of seven monolithic columns, each carrying part of a roof made of stone cut into seven blocks. The decomposition is obtained by a rigorous application of the harmonic rule contained in the golden-section rectangle; this results in a series of squares, which are disposed in a descending spiral, and which are theoretically infinite in number. In order to stop this decomposition at a practical number of squares, we set a limit at seven. Entering the room one passes from the first square of seventeen meters on a side to the seventh of seventy centimeters on a side. The continuous line that passes through the center of these squares is a spiral, the spiral that results from the topography of the *Divine Comedy,* Dante's trip across gles in gold moved visibly in the wind.

Among all these the poor woman seemed to say, "My lord, do me vengeance for my son who is slain, wherefore my heart is pierced." And he seemed to answer her, "Wait now till I return." And she, "My lord," like one whose grief is urgent, "and if you do not return?" And he, "He who shall be in my place will do it for you." And she, "What shall another's welldoing avail you, if you forget your own?" He then, "Now take comfort, for I must discharge my duty before I go: justice requires it, and pity bids me stay."
[*Purgatory* X, 73–96]

He will not feed on earth or pelf, but on wisdom, love, and virtue, and his birth shall be between felt and felt.
[*Inferno* I, 105] [N.B. This refers to the region between Feltre in the Veneto and Montefeltro in Romagna. Mussolini was born in Predappio, between these points.]

I raised my head more erect to speak, in measure as was meet; but a sight appeared which held me so fast to itself, to look on it, that I bethought me not of my confession.
[*Paradise* III, 7–9]

Plate 16 Danteum. Room of the Impero. "The
germ of the architectural whole."

the abyss of the Inferno and the mountain of Purgatory. We have thus designed a room of columns that recalls the compositional motifs of antiquity: the Orient, Greece, Italy, Egyptian rooms, Hellenic Temples, Etruscan Tombs. This adheres, then, to the thoughts of Dante that describe the moral structure of the Inferno through the Virgilian lesson of Canto XI, as if it were a reprise from a page of Aristotelian philosophy. The sensation of the *impending*, of the void formed under the crust of the earth and through a fearsome seismic disorder caused by the fall of Lucifer, can be plastically created by the overall covering of the room. This fractured ceiling and the floor, which is decomposed into diminishing squares, the scanty light that filters through the cracks in the blocks in the ceiling, all will give the catastrophic sensation of pain and useless aspiration to gain the sun and light — sensations that we find so often in the sorrowful speeches of the sinners interviewed by Dante. The seven columns, then, have thicknesses proportional to the weight they support, varying in diameter from 2.78m to .48m, resulting in an arrangement in the room that appears disorganized. The imaginary line that

128

"Cling fast," said the master, panting like a man forspent, "for by such stairs as these we must depart from so much evil."
[*Inferno* XXXIV, 82–84]

"Rise to your feet," said the master. "The way is long and the road is hard."
[*Inferno* XXXIV, 94–95]

On this side he fell down from Heaven; and the earth, which before stood out here, for fear of him made a veil of the sea and came to our hemisphere; and perhaps in order to escape from him that which appears on this side left here the empty space and rushed upwards.
[*Inferno* XXXIV, 121–123]

"Francesca, your torments make me weep for grief and pity; but tell me, in the time of the sweet sighs, by what and how did Love grant you to know the dubious desires?" And she to me, "There is no greater sorrow than to recall in wretchedness the happy time.... "
[*Inferno* V, 116–122]

129

Plate 17 Danteum. Detail of Impero. Is the eagle at the end of the promenade appearing or disappearing?

collects the group of columns in a spiral assures that such an arrangement, which is not arbitrary, will produce a sure plastic effect.

24 In the room of Purgatory, the rule of counterbalance that Dante clearly evidences in the two systems (punitive or expiatory in the two realms of Inferno and Purgatory respectively) is represented plastically by the perfect response between the floor and ceiling of each room. For the first room is provided a paving pattern that repeats the roof subdivision of seven squares, making seven steps to coincide with the seven blocks of the ceiling.

I came into a place mute of all light.
[*Inferno* V, 28]

It was no palace hall where we were, but a natural dungeon which had a bad floor and want of light.
[*Inferno* XXXIV, 96–98]

25 But it is also opportune to speak of another response that gives an exact explanation of the plastic conformity of the second room. Dante imagines Purgatory in the form of a truncated conical mountain of seven terraces or "cornices" immersed in the Australian hemisphere created by the impact of Lucifer's fall, which also created the Inferno at the opposite end of the earth, in the northern hemisphere. Purgatory is an island in a sea of water, and above the Inferno, at the opposite side (and covered by land), is the heavenly Jerusalem. We have already

brought out the parallelism between the moral topography of the Inferno and Purgatory summarized in the numerical rule of seven. It is now necessary to add the physical, material, plastic response between the *void* of the infernal chasm and the *solid* of the mystical mountain of Purgatory.

... I will sing of that second realm where the human spirit is purged and becomes fit to ascend to Heaven.
[*Purgatory* I, 4–6]

26 In designing the rooms of the Danteum we have believed it opportune to respect, with the fidelity of a performer, these fundamental concepts, reserving for ourselves a freedom of choice and synthesis in the plastic composition of the rooms. The room dedicated to the second *cantica* therefore presents analogies with the preceding room. The subdivision of the golden rectangle into seven squares is identical, but reversed in direction (to follow the itinerary that the visitor must follow). Such a concentric pattern of squares is made by a slight depression, like a valley, in the ceiling. The outline of the fascias is clearly shown — equivalent to two steps of Dante's "terraces" — which is nothing more than the proposition of the "frame" of the hypothetical structure, in terraces, of the mountain of Purgatory.

Ah, how different these passages from those of Hell, for here the entrance is with songs, and down there with fierce laments.
[*Purgatory* XII, 112–114]

He opened his arms and then spread his wings and said, "Come: the steps are at hand here, and henceforth the climb is easy."
[*Purgatory* XII, 91–93]

27 The moral "construction" of

Purgatory is incomparably simpler than that of the Inferno, and the room dedicated to Purgatory is very much more *unencumbered* and open than the preceding room. In the second *cantica* the expiation of sin through penitence gives the Poet the opportunity to present the sinners, and the allegorical scenes, with humanity, and more often with gentleness. He himself participates in the lives of the sinners, receiving on his forehead, from the spade of the Angel of the first terrace, the sign of the seven sins, which from time to time are erased by other angels, the custodians of the mountain.

"Master, tell me, what weight has been lifted from me that I feel almost no weariness as I go on?" He answered, "When the P's that are still left on your brow all but effaced shall be, as one is, quite erased, your feet shall be so conquered by good will that not only will they not feel fatigue, but it will be a delight to them to be urged upwards."
[*Purgatory* XII, 118–126]

28 The scene that we intend to prepare to properly present this second *cantica* does not omit such a poetic sensation. And by making use of the abundant light from the wide rays of sun that burst through the ample openings in the ceiling, we will succeed in creating an ambience in which the visitor feels a salutary sensation of comfort, calling his attention to the sky again, but framed by geometry....

Sweet hue of oriental sapphire which was gathering in the serene face of the sky, pure even to the first circle, to my eyes restored delight, as soon as I issued forth from the dead air that had afflicted my eyes and breast.
[*Purgatory* I, 13–18]

132

1. Editions used are: P. Toynbee, "Epistle to Can Grande," *Dantis Alagherii Epistolae* (Oxford: Clarendon Press, 1922); *Divine Comedy*, Charles S. Singleton, trans. (Princeton: Princeton University Press, 1970); the Penguin edition of *Vita Nuova;* and *De Monarchia*, trans. from the Penguin *Purgatory.*

O you who have sound understanding, mark the doctrine that is hidden under the veil of strange verses.
Dante, Inferno *IX*

TERRAGNI AND DANTE

AS THE PARALLELS BETWEEN THE RELAZIONE and Dante's works explain, Terragni's identification with his literary predecessor ran deep; so deep, in fact, that an exploration into the connections between building and poem, architect and poet, seems imperative if we are to fathom the complete meaning of the Danteum project.

Terragni's propensity to cross-reference architecture and literature, almost to the point of confusing the two, may have been due to his friendship with Massimo Bontempelli. [1] This literary figure was a great influence on the painters and architects of the modern movement in Italy, and as editor of *Quadrante,* the multidisciplinary review, Bontempelli was able to bring together people from all the arts — literary, plastic, and theatrical. Architecture as a form of language *(linguaggio)* was one of Bontempelli's primary interests, and his dictum "Write without adjectives, build with smooth walls" [2] — futurist in origin — is a prime example of the potential interconnection between the two media. He makes clear his interest in such cross-referencing and cross-fertilization:

> Speaking of poetry (or art in general) as architecture I mean to say art as a modification of the inhabitable world.... The principal consequence of the particular nature of the work of

architecture is the absolute detachment of the work itself from its author. The work is a real and actual alteration of the earth's crust.... The architectonic work may be great even if the authors don't know it.... The *estrangement* of the work from the author, this perfect cutting of the umbilical cord in literature, happens with the creation of myths, of fables, of characters.... This must be our supreme ideal, fellow writers: to become anonymous. [3]

If poetry, or literature in general, may borrow the technique of anonymity from architecture, then the architect may also emulate the writer. To Terragni this meant the creation, in an architectural composition, of myths and characters. In the Danteum and the *Relazione* he academically separated form from content, myth from composition, so that the two might be fused again in the act of designing.

Terragni also borrowed ideas on form and content from Benedetto Croce. The relation of subject matter, whether Dante and the *Comedy* or traditional architectural elements like columns and porticos, to the abstract structure of an architectural composition was a problem that constantly intrigued Terragni. Croce as well considered the problem in *Aesthetic* (1902). According to Croce the response to conventional elements within abstract compositions comes from the intuitive activity of the mind. For Croce, intuitive knowledge, or the aesthetic, is "the first grade on which other grades of activity depend." [4] The premise for this is the separation between "grafted meaning" (Terragni's term) and intuition of the compositional structure of the building. The ultimate response to the project would require no intellectual activity on the part of the observer, even though the geometry of Terragni's composition is filled with intellectual manipulations. He made no claim for the immediate perception of the formal transformations that he explained existed in the building's composition. Terragni was more interested in a purely historical set of references.

Croce equates *intuition* and *expression,* claiming that in the synthesis of artistic achievement it is such *expression* that forms the germ of the work — distinguishing the work of the artist from that of the scientist. For Croce, and Terragni after him,

Matter, clothed and conquered by form, produces concrete form. It is matter, the content, which differentiates one of our intuitions from another; the form is constant; it is spiritual activity, while matter is changeable. Without matter spiritual activity would not forsake its abstractness to become concrete and real activity, this or that spiritual content, this or that definite intuition. [5]

For Terragni, then, forms are desirable because they adhere to "harmonic law" (his term); they are communicative because they are overlaid with a semantic intention. Thus, while Bontempelli argued for the adaptation of architectural modes of thought, Terragni, with his ability to stretch the notion of correspondence to the breaking point, easily adopted the literary theme as the program or *content* for the Danteum; i.e., the subject matter of his composition. In the modern movement of the 1930s this was something of a revolutionary act.

The interest in literary texts, in an architecture *of* literature, was not to become an issue again until the seventies, with the parallel interest in architecture as text, which was researched by the semiologists. As late as 1968 Terragni's intended architecture-of-literature was criticized by Giulio Carlo Argan, dean of Italian architectural historians. According to Argan, the Danteum was "an enormous mistake: the idea of making a correspondence between the plan distribution of a building and the structure of a poem is almost comical, but not more than the intention of architecturally expressing victory, patriotism, or the longevity of the Empire." [6] Argan's arguments might have been rebutted by Terragni, or even by Bontempelli, with historical examples of buildings used as systems of memory in the same way that literature codifies memory. Hadrian's Villa, medieval cathedrals, and Renaissance gardens were all such architectures. Furthermore, the notion of expressing the longevity of the Empire would certainly be accepted by any modern critic, Argan included, as a reasonable intention of the ancient Romans.

The *Divine Comedy* was itself a kind of memory book for Divine Grace and how to achieve it, as Frances Yates has demonstrated so eloquently. [7] The *Comedy* also describes one of the most elaborate architectural promenades in all of literature. To build a Danteum (more than just a Dante museum and study center) would be no more upsetting, I believe, to the sensibility of modern Italians than making a film of the poem.

Terragni is further indebted to Croce for the latter's interpretation of Dante, an interpretation that divides Dante's form from his content,

137

arguing that Dante's poetic imagination could be appreciated in an *analytical* way. [8] Any problems inherent in such an approach can be overcome, says Croce,

> ... only by making a sharp distinction between structure and poetry, placing them to be sure in strict philosophical and ethical relationship and thereby considering them necessary elements of Dante's spirit, but being careful to avoid any idea of a poetical relationship between them. Only in this way is it possible to enjoy all of the poetry of the *Commedia* profoundly and at the same time accept its structure, with some indifference perhaps, but without aversion and, above all, without derision.[9]

Without derision indeed! Rather, for Terragni the appreciation of Dante's structure, with the aid of Croce's lens, could lead to an adaptation of that structure irrespective of matter. It is almost as if Croce had given Terragni the green light to deal with Dante's numerology on the one hand and his allegory on the other, all the time using different criteria for his selection of images. Hence, Terragni could claim that "architectural monument and literary work can adhere to a singular scheme ... only through an examination of the admirable structure of the Divine Poem." [10] For Terragni the Poem's structure had to exist independently, applicable to either the Poem or the building; otherwise the Danteum would be *dependent* on the Poem and unable to "confront" it on equal footing. Terragni thus presents us with an implied argument for the importance of architecture in society that is similar to Dante's argument for the importance of poetry in the late Middle Ages.[11]

Terragni cautioned against making the monument a too-exact copy of the ambience of the Poem. Yet he ran the same risk as Croce: an arbitrary separation of the components of an artwork that otherwise forms an indelible gestalt. Croce himself was criticized by Pirandello for this very "fault":

> If he [Dante] wrote the *Commedia,* this indicates that he did not want to write a treatise or a work composed of poetical and nonpoetical parts; but a poem.... His [Dante's] fantasy is populated with images and not ideas. But Croce says that "subject matter" in Dante's spirit "is shaped by poetry" and then remains subject matter for an allegorico-moral treatise. [12]

It would seem that Terragni's concept of Dante, at least as regards the Danteum design, makes the *Commedia* into just such a hypothetical *treatise,* enabling Terragni to analyze its component parts and pick and choose certain architecturally relevant aspects to imitate.

The resulting transposition of concepts from one medium to another was important enough for Terragni to dwell upon it at great length in the *Relazione.* The transposition may be seen as his ultimate escape from both the functionalist rigors of the International Style and the "subservient" (his term) copy-book eclecticism of the Piacentiniani. If we reverse Bontempelli's dictum to read "to build without adjectives," the question for Terragni becomes, "What constitutes a proper architectural adjective? Can the rhetorical Roman details of the Piacentiniani be considered reasonable, or are they more akin to Alberti's idea of decoration as the adjunct to beauty?"

Terragni's idea of an architectural adjective would embrace any architectural element that does *not* directly derive from the central themes of a building, something "added" in the Albertian sense; hence, Terragni insisted on maintaining a singular theme in the Danteum design so as to create an architecture without adjective. The development of subthemes would permit the use of adjectives as additives in the design process, as we see in the Casa Giuliani-Frigerio, a building that Lingeri said contained "enough ideas for forty houses." [13] Most certainly Terragni's idea of an architectural adjective organic to the design would not allow the superimposition of the arches and columns that Ojetti had proposed as necessary elements of an Italian architecture. [14] The Danteum, as a didactic building, had to be far simpler on this level to avoid what Terragni called the possibility of "falling into rhetoricism, into symbolism, or into convention." [15]

WHATEVER THE REASONS FOR TERRAGNI'S OBSESsive identification with Dante, it allowed him to adopt the strategies of the medieval poet. His identification manifested itself in various ways. It is first revealed in Terragni's writing style in the *Relazione,* a mirror of Dante's style, and in the format of the *Relazione.* In this report Terragni makes reference to the *Convivio* and *De Monarchia,* explaining that the allusions to the longevity of the Roman Empire were first expounded in these books, and this building, being dedicated to Dante and all his works, might derive from the early works of the *dolce stil nuovo*. Dante's concept of the Empire, with the Emperor receiving his just sovereignty over the secular world directly from God, with the Church receiving its power over the spirit without being superior in any way to the Empire, was of course crucial to Mussolini's Italy. Terragni, a devout Catholic, might well have been able to resolve the problem of the Church of Rome through Dante; the fascists certainly did. Moreover, it was Dante's concept of the Roman Empire that made him the cultural hero he was — in an Italy that, during the fascist era, had diminished the importance of the Middle Ages.

Essential to Terragni's *Relazione* was Dante's own "Relazione," his *Epistle to Can Grande Della Scala*. The *Epistle to Can Grande* was a letter of thanks for hospitality, an offering of the *Paradise* as a present to the nobleman, and a brief explanation of the meanings of the *Paradise* (and the entire *Comedy*), lest they be lost in a difficult text filled with many levels of allegory. The letter was a guide to the structure of the Poem, the different "senses" of the structure and content, and the explanation of Dante's choices for the different types of exposition. The *Relazione* is exactly this sort of document. It was clearly Terragni's "Epistle to Mussolini"; and while one must here conflate Can Grande, the patron, with Henry of Luxembourg, the "Greyhound," in order to arrive at the figure of Mussolini, this is not an act beyond Terragni's imagination.

Dante first divided form from content, or structure from meaning. He explains the form of the Poem in terms of a descending series of structural elements, as Terragni does for the Danteum when he writes, "the mathematical and geometric correspondences can be traced in turn for the most important divisions of the rooms of the building — deriving the workings of the plan from the decomposition of the golden rectangle." [16] Dante divided the form of the treatise into three: 1) the three *canticas*, 2) the division of each *cantica* into cantos, and 3) the division of each canto into rhymed lines. [17] The *treatment,* which Dante explains as the second part of a "twofold" form, is subdivided into ten types: "poetic, fictive, descriptive, digressive, figurative; and further, definitive, analytical, probative, refutative, and explicative." [18] Dante thus plays with twofold versus threefold divisions, an idea that is reflected in the divisions of the Danteum. The cruciform scheme that makes twofold divisions compares to the tripartite division of the building.

Terragni elaborated his version of the play of twofold and threefold division in his intention to gain "unity in trinity." He even digressed into an arcane explanation of the golden rectangle as the "rectangle that clearly expresses the harmonic law of unity in trinity," with the further explanation that "*one* is the rectangle, *three* are the segments that determine the golden ratio." [19] Terragni explained that the creation of an infinite number of squares and rectangles in the decomposition of the golden rectangle, causing a spiral form, has a Dantesque significance: the concept of the infinite. He also used the spiral motif in the composition of the Inferno and the Purgatory as flat projections of the funnel and conical forms of Dante's domains.

In the *Relazione* Terragni's division of structure and meaning, i.e., his geometry and what it represents, further parallels the *Epistle* in format; his insistence on using the same scheme for the first compositional decisions as for the details also recalls Dante: "In like manner the form of the part is determined by that of the whole work." [20]

The pragmatic character of progression (or promenade) in the *Paradise* is reflected in the Danteum design. Dante explains, "The process of narrative will be ascent from heaven to heaven." [21] Terragni explains, "A tripartite Temple of rooms disposed at different levels establishes an ascending route." [22] The key phrase in Terragni's adaptation of Dante's ideas then follows: "Constructed in different ways, these rooms are integrated to gradually prepare the visitor for a sublimination of matter and light." [23] The sentence is most Dantesque and paraphrases the origin of poetry according to St. Augustine, who, like Dante after him, had read Virgil. Poetry, according to Augustine, was "the first notion of a rational soul trying to reach beyond the world of matter and change." [24]

Transcendence is an essential quality of the *Comedy* and the Danteum. The decomposition of the golden rectangle and the decomposition of the materiality of the Paradise together express the notion. Dante was careful to distinguish sequential experience from deeper significance, as in the *Paradise*, where, because he is "in his first life, impeded by the limitations of mortality, he cannot see things in their essence, as the blessed do, but only in their sequence, which is how he has shown them." [25] The Divine Law is not revealed in sequence, nor is the structure of the Poem. One must step back, as it were, and gaze at the work from some distance to understand its complete rule and essence. In the Danteum only the most obvious of Dante's structural motifs, aside from the rendering of the spaces dedicated to the *canticas* of the poem, are revealed in the sequence. The rest is left to a reading of the plan and, I believe, the *Relazione*. The document, like the *Epistle*, forms the footnotes, the key to the intentions of the author.

The obfuscation of the actual generating structure of the building is an important intention for Terragni; it is clear that a good deal of effort is required of the participant to unravel the experience. Dante's own warnings on the difficulties of his poem (and hence the attainment of beatitude) parallel those of Terragni. In Canto X of *Paradise* he writes:

> Now remain, reader, upon your bench, reflecting
> on this of which you have a foretaste,
> if you would be glad far sooner than wary.
> I have set before you; now feed yourself,
> because that matter of which I am made the
> scribe wrests to itself all my care. [26]

The visitor is, after all, a "pilgrim" who must enter the sacred domain as any pilgrim would enter a pilgrimage church, with at least a modicum of acceptance, prior knowledge, and a purposeful intent.

The independence of the essence from the sequence manifests itself in the geometry of the building as the shifted rectangle and the golden section. These are *abstracted* forms, similar to the abstracted forms of the structure of the *Comedy*. Terragni is quick to remind us that abstraction alone can lead to relevant and justifiable results:

> The connection between the plastic-architectonic expression and the abstraction and symbolism of the theme of the building (a connection that could cast doubt on the relevance and spontaneity of the results) was only possible at the *origin* of those two discrete spiritual facts: building and poem. Architectural monument and literary work can adhere to a *singular* scheme without losing, in this union, any of each work's essential qualities only if both possess a structure and a harmonic rule that can allow them to confront each other, so that they may then be read in a geometric or mathematical relation of parallelism or

subordination. [27]

Abstraction as an active process, however, begins with the concrete, the real in a secular sense, and leads to a conceptual synthesis, unlike simple pattern-making. Abstracting presupposes not only an original form but to some degree an original form-meaning combination, resulting in a dialogue between the old and the new meanings. As the Gestalt psychologist Frederick Perls states, "Meaning is the relation between the foreground figure and its background." [28] Terragni uses the concept in a way that is similar to, but not the same as, Le Corbusier's idea that "between the chosen theme object and the plastic organism ... there intervenes the necessary labor of total plastic recreation." [29] In other words, this is Croce's "concrete intuition" made manifest by virtue of the active process. To Le Corbusier the process of recreation involves mathematics and geometry in order to arrive at the most essential *aesthetic* experience. "Pure forms are the most beautiful because they are the most easily perceived." [30] The famous mathematical, geometric forms of Corbusier's sketches are emblematic of this aesthetic experience. For Terragni the experience is *metaphysical*. It is closer to that of Mies, as Steven Peterson has indicated in his seminal essay on meaning in Mies. [31] The *rectangle* itself represents the most abstract condition, as shown by the equal rectangles used to depict the *canticas* of the *Comedy,* which are so different in size and shape in Dante's text.

143

Terragni's abstraction of architectural elements into an architectonic code never results in the destruction of those elements. The form of an element in the *Divine Comedy* may be a "three-line tercet"; the form of an element in the building may be a cylinder. The cylinder may also be a column, which not only functions as a support but possesses a tradition of use. The column in a series produces a "portico" (Terragni's term), further elaborating the grammar of elements. Thus, the convergence of two methods of abstraction, the first originating in an abstract form — the golden rectangle — the second originating in traditional architectural objects, finds justification in Dante.

The notion of separating essence from sequence did not explain Terragni's identification with Dante. A symbolic purpose for the convergence of these methods was necessary. Terragni gave thought, for example, to choosing the rectangle as the most rudimentary thematic element of the building. He was concerned about the appropriate form to be selected and began the *Relazione* with a justification for the golden section, beginning with a disclaimer that the circle was discarded at first "because the area it encloses is too modest for what was needed, but also because of the immediacy of potential conflict with the perfect and imposing ellipse of the Colosseum." [32]

On the other hand, Terragni perceived the rectangle as abstract as the circle, even if the circle were a higher form in the cosmic order. It was likewise necessary for the Danteum to be both an abstract construction as well as the embodiment of "myths and commonly held symbols," involving a "spiritual synthesis." [33] (Terragni's need to create a symbolic architecture of connotative significance was well established by the time he had completed the Casa del Fascio in Como, his "glass house of Fascism.")

While historical justification was important to Terragni, a Dantesque justification was *necessary;* and the more Dantesque motifs he could conjure the better. He assumed the position, often attributed to Le Corbusier, that the more reasons one can find for a given decision, the better the decision. Terragni's justification of the circle changed to the rectangle is typical of the kind of analogue to Dante that he used. In the *Paradise* we find Dante grappling with the question of the relation of the square to the circle, using it for his own poetic purposes:

As the geometer his mind applies
to square the circle, nor for all his wit
finds the right way, how'er he tries. [34]

For Dante this explains the immeasurability of the circle in terms of the square and therefore represents man's inability to come to terms with the ineffable, the image of God. [35] Man is the square, God the circle. The relationship of the two geometric figures bears the added characteristic of the architectonic opposition as an expression of traditional opposites, the circular versus the rectangular temple, the nave versus the apse, etc. The circle is at once more concrete and more abstract, as the form of the columns and as the motif of spiral in the Inferno and Purgatory. The rectangle then becomes the carrier of whatever "grafted meaning" may be appropriate, as well as the origin of all correctness, of rationale. He begins the design with a given form, the golden rectangle. The way he receives this form, as if it were God-given, is similar to Dante's assertion that "every motion, but the First, is caused." [36] Terragni was careful to explain that the manipulations of the golden rectangle were still insufficient to explain the meaning of the Danteum in terms of Dante. The ultimate purpose for Terragni's Dantesque correspondences is revealed in the *Epistle to Can Grande,* a thought Terragni might have borrowed from his medieval mentor:

> The meaning of this work is not of one kind only; rather the work may be described as having several meanings; for the first meaning is that which is conveyed by the letter, and the next by which the letter signifies; the former is called the literal while the latter is called allegorical, or mystical. [37]

For Terragni the meaning was manifested in what he called "research into essentials," an arcane digression on medieval thought relating his own process to that of Dante. These concepts derive from medieval fourfold exegesis. It is necessary to discuss Terragni's conceptualization of these ideas.

The categories of fourfold exegesis are the literal, allegorical, moral, and anagogical. How these categories fit together — their inner structure — was of great importance to Dante and Terragni. In the simplest terms, "The literal teaches the deeds, the allegory what to believe, the moral what to do, and the anagoge whereto you should strive." [38] Dante had grappled with the problem of how the categories related to each other in a twofold manner and fourfold manner. In the twofold system the literal is contrasted to the allegorical, which subsumes the moral and anagogical senses. This was Dante's schema in the *Epistle to Can Grande.* In the *Convivio* Dante had adhered to the more elaborate fourfold division, where all senses are given equal footing.

By contrast Terragni simplified the readings of the exegesis by making a threefold division, perhaps an attempt to follow his tripartite divisions of the building itself. Whatever the motive, he contrasts the literal, the allegorical, and the anagogical. [39] The literal sense of the *Comedy* is an architectural promenade, according to Terragni. It is the "subterranean trip" that parallels the travels of Saint Paul and other pilgrimages of discovery. The allegorical sense of the *Comedy,* according to Terragni, is Dante as the personification of "the [moral] amelioration of ... sinful humanity." [40] Terragni defines the anagogical sense as the installation of the Empire:

The *anagogical* sense is the vision of eternal happiness ... of the Roman Empire with its center in Rome, for worldly prosperity, and [moral] restoration of the Church ... liberated from the temporal power that pollutes it — for spiritual happiness, with its center also in Rome. [41]

Terragni's particularization of Dante's anagogical sense was typical of fascist thought and might even be construed as pandering to the regime. Seizing the opportunity to justify his buildings in Dantesque terms, Terragni further explained the "didactic" quality of the work as an almost unnecessary symbol of the already reestablished Roman Empire. It was mere confirmation of "Dante's 'dowry' of prophecy." [42]

Terragni neglects to add his interpretation of the "senses" of exegesis as regards the building; however, he hints that such an interpretation would be logical. After all, if the Danteum were to embody the principles of the *Divine Comedy,* it would be logical that it be based on the *meanings* of the *Comedy* as well. It is necessary, I believe, to interpret these levels of significance in order to understand Terragni's thought and the extent of his symbolic activity, which in turn throws light on his apparent abstraction and the relationship of figurative to abstract art.

The conflation of the modes of exegesis found in Dante's two texts shows that Terragni, like Dante, was concerned with "distinguishing the allegorical from the literal sense.... " [43] The literal "sense" of the Danteum as a representational object (not its architectonic "presence") is patently Dante, not just the *Comedy.* It is Dante of the early works as well, with the forecourt representing the life of Dante before his "trip." The walls, columns, floors, etc., are to Dante's person what Dante's words were to "the state of souls after death, pure and simple." [44] Terragni was careful to place in context any references to Dante, the context being architecturally historical and political. While the composition of the building was to be "spiritually chained to Dantesque compositional criteria," it was likewise necessary that "the meaning of the symbol ... not obscure the effective plastic necessity ... [and] that we have already resolved the problems of volumetric equilibrium and architectonic harmony." [45] The literal meaning, like Dante's, is topical and must be augmented by the allegorical meaning.

It is interesting to note here the parallel between Dante's and Terragni's respective invocations of history and precedent. Dante peopled his *Comedy* with real historical characters and then superseded time and place, making "all-time and all-place," allowing the reader to relate these specific events of his journey to the cosmos. Dante further invoked history in terms of the longevity of the Empire and dealt with his own identity problem as a poet in the Middle Ages. Nancy Lenkeith summarizes this problem:

> To defend Rome and the Roman way of life, Dante had to defend himself as a poet.... A long disparagement of poetry had followed the decay of Roman culture.... The fact is that poetry and poets were not essential to the Christian scheme of saving the world. [46]

For architects under fascism the problem was analagous. Although they led themselves to believe, as did architects all over Europe, that they were central in shaping the future, the regime was careful to let the architects argue among themselves and accomplish very little in terms of social benefits. Yet throughout the thirties, even when the battle for modern design as the official style of the regime had more or less failed, architects like Terragni, Pagano, Sartoris, and others tried to convince the regime of its benefits. Terragni's text here reads like a kind of latter-day version of Pietro Maria Bardi's *Rapporto Sul Architettura* to Mussolini, an attempt to convince the Duce of the capacity of modern architecture to symbolize the revolutionary qualities of the fascist state (albeit Terragni's text has none of the bile of Bardi's polemic). [47]

It seems reasonable to assume, then, that since Terragni was preoccupied with explaining the senses of the *Comedy*, the Danteum would display a similar aim. Hence, if Dante's mathematics and atmosphere were appropriate to render in stone, then why not his allegory? At any rate, the literal reading of both building and poem, *while still important,* would be insufficient to either author.

Neither can the literal meaning for both authors be interpreted simply as the inadequate metaphor of a higher level of thought; the question of how allegory is used must be of some interest to us here. An allegory of "this for that," one that presupposes that "objects of perception have value only as they lead us toward the ineffable ... the inadequate signs of ideas," is the spirit of gnosticism, which some scholars argue that Dante adjured. [48] These scholars believe that Dante was concerned with an allegory of "this *and* that," giving greater importance to even the literal, but certainly to the allegorical and moral senses, rather than placing all emphasis on the anagoge.

A simple abstract reading of the Danteum cannot express Terragni's desire to create so many rich levels of meaning in a disarmingly simple project. The "clues to the spiritualized, nontangible abstract essence of the universe" are themselves objects of interest and importance. [49] They become for Dante and Terragni what Max Black calls "interaction metaphors," where the simultaneous reading of the metaphor and its "frame" creates its particular meaning. [50] One can thus refer to Zuccoli's paraphrase of Terragni's design theory: "Architecture is never only a composition of elements in certain relationships; it is a house, a school, an airport, etc." [51]

The broad range of meanings of the Danteum are a direct reflection, if not a conscious copying, of Dante's "form, or manner ... [which is] ... poetic, fictive, digressive," etc. [52] In the Danteum it is the column (*figure 92*) that absorbs so many levels of metaphor; it is the generic architectonic element, a kind of lowest common denominator of concrete "parts." The column is a cylinder: pure geometry. As historical allusions, the Danteum columns may be Terragni's version of Dante's "coupling of a Christian and a pagan source in order to clarify a contemporary event."

For instance, the Danteum columns are at once the plain cylinders of Le Corbusier's *piloti* and the columns of classical antiquity, proportioned like the Doric order, complete with capitals and lacking only *entasis*. They are *all the columns that ever were*. They are also the circle, symbol of perfection and the highest form of geometric figure. In series, the columns become a portico, with a pediment in the form of the fractured wall they support. In clusters they stand for the ritual of initiation and route of purification well known through the revival of Egyptian forms in the lodges of the eighteenth century. [53] The column is the umbrella of shelter for the poor souls of the Inferno; it is the symbol of infinity (and therefore eternity) as the glass column of the *Paradise,* as well as the reference to futurism and *Glass Architektur.* The transparency of the column coincides with Dante's concept of transparency in Paradise. That is, through transparency all Divine Grace is

148

revealed. Dante wrote in the *Convivio* that " ... the excellence of God
is received in one way by separate substances, that is, by angels, who are
free from all coarseness of matter, being, as it were, transparent by
reason of the purity of their form." [54] Hence form is made manifest by
its dissection, as in Terragni's dissection of the column through its cry-
stalline character, as in the dissection of the floors, walls, and ceiling of
the Paradise, resulting in the abstracting of the space away from its corporeal concreteness. As a reference to the *Comedy* the column reflects
its numerology as the 100 cantos of the complete work, the thirty-three
cantos of the Paradise, and the seven divisions of the Inferno.

The columns, walls, and beams are "this *and* that." Dante thus
provided a model of organization that eschews a simple binary distinction between the literal and the allegorical. His overlapping categories
of treatment, from reference through connotation to invocation, provided Terragni a foothold for his own design activity and for his epistle
to Mussolini, the *Relazione*.

To return to the representational "senses" of the Danteum, I would
propose that the allegorical sense relates to the participant's experience
of the reattainment of the Roman Empire, hence the addition of the
room dedicated to the Empire. The Danteum was in this regard like
the Casa del Fascio in Como: the Glass and Marble House of Fascism.
The Empire was to Terragni and Dante *a living thing,* having
"repented" to reemerge in Terragni's time as Dante had prophesied.
Or, in Dante's terms, "The Phoenix dies and is reborn from fire." [55]

An anagogical sense for the Danteum, however, requires some
speculation because it involves the conflation of the mystical and the
spiritual, with the spiritual pertaining to an immaterial reality. The first
clue to Terragni's anagogical "intent," therefore, is perhaps his concept
of the building as a synthetic type created from the types he discarded:
the museum, the palace, and the theater. He considered the Danteum a
temple, a building type that combines all the functions of the others,
but one that transcends their expressive capabilities. In the "secular"
terms of geometry and architectural forms this requires the transcendence of materials, functions, and arrangements (columns, stone,
rooms, etc.). [56] It is a transcendence that recalls the ineffably beautiful
vision of God from the *Paradise:*

Strove I with that wonder, how to fit

149

150

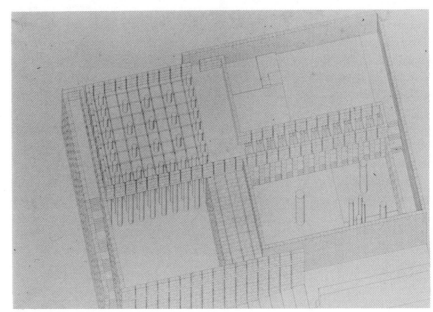

92 Danteum. Axonometric, detail of the portico.

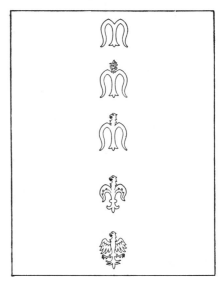

93 Transformation of the letter *M* into the image of the eagle.

the image to the sphere; so sought to see

How is maintained the point of rest in it. [57]

The reality of this experience, the attainment of which required Dante to traverse the depths of hell and travel through Purgatory and Paradise, is parallel to Terragni's elimination of all but the most rudimentary of architectonic rules. The Danteum, in its complete plastic reality, with an architectural structure that mirrors the structure of heaven, with a purity of such high order that all profane objects drop away, confronts us with an otherworldliness that seems to counteract all laws of man and nature. If the inclusion of, and the design intentions for, the space of the Impero may signal the allegorical sense of the Danteum, then the design of the Paradise must surely signal the anagogical sense, if indeed we may speak of such architectural meanings in this way.

The act of abstracting these spaces allows Terragni to have his room and to deny it, to have his literal and anagogical senses confront each other. Typical of Terragni's use of his model is the image of the eagle that adorns the end wall of the Impero (*plate 17*). The eagle refers directly to the transformation of the letter *M* into the image of the eagle in Canto XVIII of the *Paradise*. The eagle, symbol of imperial justice, appears as a transformation of the last letter of the phrase *Diligite Justitian Qui Judicatis Terram* (*figure 93*) ("He who rules the earth should seek justice," a phrase that conveniently contains thirty-five letters, Dante's age upon "entering" the *Comedy* and Terragni's age when he designed the Danteum, and the product of the numbers five and seven). [58] Dante's reference to the nullification of the temporal powers of the papacy and the installation of the Empire is the most overt symbol of this painted eagle. The rendering of the image recalls Dante's verses in the way the image rests on the drawing almost as if an afterthought, a supplement to the Sironi reliefs that were to adorn the facades. The letter *M* is also for Mussolini, who often signed documents with a big *M*.

Thus Terragni's treatment is expansive, like Dante's, as shown in the format and style of the building and the *Relazione*. Both are atmospheric, connotative, denotative, referential, correspondent, and embrace a continuum from form to content. But before I can conclude with what appears to be a total correspondence between building and poem,

151

I am compelled to repeat Terragni's caveat:

> Architectural monument and literary work can adhere to a *singular* theme without losing, in this union, any of each work's essential qualities only if *both* [my italics] possess a structure and a harmonic rule that allow them to confront each other.... [59]

Terragni assures us that while the building is about Dante and his poem, it is not merely the *Comedy* rendered in stone. For Terragni, architectural themes do not grow out of the subject matter to which they adhere, but instead are independent in origin. Neither pragmatic functions nor institutional symbolic intentions can create architectural forms; nor is the "literal" sense of a building on its own terms a mere similacrum of the literal story of a work of literature. Terragni's project is text-dependent for its symbolic meaning only. [60] As a work of architecture, it remains autonomous.

In 1949, six years after Terragni's tragic death, Le Corbusier was invited to cut the ribbon for the opening of a Terragni retrospective in Como. As he toured the show, Le Corbusier stopped only once — in front of the Danteum panels. He knew nothing of the commission, the *Relazione,* or the context of the work. He was moved to exclaim, "This is the work of an Architect."

152

1. For a discussion of Bontempelli's influence on modern architecture in Italy and on Terragni, see A. Longatti, "Massimo Bontempelli e l'architettura 'naturale,'" *L'Architettura* 163 (May 1969), 34–36.

2. Ibid.

3. Ibid., 34.

4. Herbert Carr, *The Philosophy of Benedetto Croce* (New York: Russel and Russel, 1969).

5. Benedetto Croce, *Aesthetic* (Bari: Laterza, 1902), 6.

6. Argan, "Relazione," *L'Architettura* 163, 7.

7. Frances Yates, *The Art of Memory* (London: Routledge & K. Paul, 1966).

8. Croce, *La Poesia di Dante* (Bari: Laterza, 1921).

9. Ibid., quoted in John Freccero ed., *Dante, A Collection of Critical Essays* (Englewood Cliffs, NJ: Prentice-Hall, 1965), 14.

10. Relazione, para. 5.

11. See chap. 4.

12. Quoted in Freccero, *Dante, A Collection,* 20.

13. Taken from my interview with Piercarlo Lingeri.

14. For the debate on "Arches and Columns" between Ugo Ojetti and Marcello Piacentini, see Patetta, *Architettura in Italia.*

15. Relazione, para. 8.

16. Ibid., para. 11.

17. See Paget Toynbee, *Dantis Alagherii Epistolae* (Oxford: Clarendon Press, 1922), for a translation of Dante's *Epistle to Can Grande Della Scala.*

18. Ibid.

19. Relazione, para. 6.

20. Epistle to Can Grande, para. 12.

21. Ibid., para. 33.

22. Relazione, para. 23.

23. Ibid.

24. Nancy Lenkeith, "Dante and the Idea of Rome," *Journal of the Warburg Institute* (London: 1952), 32.

25. Barbara Reynolds, "Introduction," in Dante Alighieri, *Paradise,* (London: Penguin, 1962), 26.

26. Dante, *Divine Comedy,* Canto X, 22–27.

27. Relazione, para. 5.

28. Frederick Perls, *Gestalt Therapy Verbatim* (New York: Books That Matter, 1970), 12.

29. Le Corbusier and A. Ozenfant, *Esprit Nouveau* 4.

30. Charles-Edouard Jeanneret-Gris, *Towards a New Architecture,* by Le Corbusier, trans. Frederick Etchells (New York: Praeger, 1970), 26.

31. Steven K. Peterson, "A Mies Understanding," *The Inland Architect* (Spring 1977).

32. Relazione, para. 3.

33. Ibid., para. 4.

34. Paradise, Canto XXXIII.

35. Reynolds, introduction to *Paradise.*

36. Epistle to Can Grande, para. 21.

37. Ibid., para. 7.

38. Robert Hollander, quoting Aquinas, *Allegory in Dante's Commedia* (Princeton: Princeton University Press, 1969), 28.

39. In the manuscript the word is misspelled as *analogico,* but Terragni's explanation is so close to Dante's that there can be no doubt that he meant *anagogical.* The mistake must be attributed to typing or to infrequent use of the word *anagogical* in this century.

40. Relazione, para. 19.

41. Ibid.

42. Ibid., para 20.

43. Reynolds, introduction to *Paradise,* para. 47.

44. Epistle to Can Grande, para. 8.

45. Relazione, para. 10.

46. Lenkeith, "Dante and the Idea," 33.

47. Pietro Maria Bardi, *Rapporto Sul Architettura* (Rome: 1931).

48. Hollander, *Allegory,* 5.

49. Ibid.

50. Max Black, *Models and Metaphors, Studies in Language and Philosophy* (Ithaca: Cornell University Press, 1962).

51. Zuccoli, *L'Architettura* 163.

52. Epistle to Can Grande.

53. See Anthony Vidler, "The Architecture of the Lodges," *Oppositions* 5 (Summer 1976).

54. Dante Alighieri, *Convivio,* Tractate III, vii, trans. William Walpond Jackson (Oxford: Clarendon Press, 1909), 18–57.

55. Paradise, Canto XXIV.

56. The similarity between Terragni and the de Stijl movement is unmistakable. Mondrian and Van Doesburg were influenced by

153

the mystical mathematician Schoonmakers, who believed that in the geometry of the right angle was the key to the essence of the universe. See H. C. L. Jaffe, *de Stijl.*

57. *Paradise,* Canto XXXIII.

58. See W. Vernon, *Readings on the Paradise of Dante* (New York: Macmillan, 1900), 32–61. It is a significant coincidence that Terragni was in his thirty-fifth year when he designed the Danteum. One suspects that this fact contributed to his inordinate identification with Dante.

59. *Relazione,* para. 5.

60. The term "text-dependent architecture" is a term used by Judith Wolin in various contexts relating architecture to literature.

154

DOCUMENTS

Rino Valdameri, **The Danteum Statute, 1938**

1 A "Danteum" is to be created in Rome: A National Organization that proposes to erect, on the Via dell'Impero, in this epoch, in which the will and genius of the Duce have realized the Imperial dream of Dante, a Temple to the greatest of Italian poets.

2 The Danteum is proposed to:

a) carry out the celebration of the words of Dante, considered a primary source for Mussolini's creations;

b) aid in its continuous dissemination;

c) construct a library complete with all that is needed for students of Dante; to keep in its collection all the illustrations totally or partially inspired by the *Commedia* and the *Vita Nuova,* and all that is of interest to the iconography of the poet;

d) promote in Italy and foreign lands courses on Dante, to become the living center of any studies and research related to the works of the poet;

e) to suggest and aid those initiatives that foster and attest to the character of Imperial Fascist Italy.

3 The Organization will be under the vigilance of the Head of State, First Minister, Secretary of State. It will be directed by a Directorship of twenty members, composed of the following officers: the National Minister of Education, the Minister of Popular Culture, the Minister of Finance, the representative of the Directorship of the National Fascist Party (PNF), the representative of the National Fascist Institute of Culture, the President of the royal Italian Academy, the Mayor of the city of Rome, the President of the National Dante Society, the President of the Italian Dante Society [Valdameri himself]. The President and the members of the Directorship are nominated by the chief of the Government. They will serve five years. The President is chief of the Organization and as such he assumes all its social powers. From among the members of the Directorship will be selected the General Secretary, to whom is entrusted the Organization and the development of the activities of the Organization according to the directives of the President.

4 The Directorship assists the President in governing the Association. The Directorship will be convened by the President whenever he deems it necessary, but at least once every three months. The President and

the members of the Directorship serve without pay. The Directorship will convene in Rome, at the Danteum.

5 The President will submit for approval of the Head of Government and Prime Minister, Secretary of State, the rules and regulations of the present Statute.

Letter from Rino Valdameri to Osvaldo Sebastiani *[personal secretary to Mussolini]*
19 October 1938
Milano, 19 October 1938 XVI
Excellency,

In conformity with the wishes of His Excellency the Head of State, and in agreement with (Gr. Uff.) [Grand Official] Alessandro Poss, I have had the architects Giuseppe Terragni and Pietro Lingeri prepare the Danteum project, to be built along the Street of the Empire (Via dell'Impero) in Rome.

Begging your pardon for interrupting your important duties, I wish to request from the Head of State an audience with myself, Poss, and the Architects Terragni and Lingeri, where we may furnish the Duce a clear and detailed project description for the Head of State to examine.

At the same time, in reference to a past promise, Alessandro Poss will offer to His Excellency, the Head of State, the sum of two million lire as his personal contribution toward the erection of the Danteum.

Please accept, Excellency, my cordial devoted Fascist regards,
Rino Valdameri
Piazza Boromeo 7

Telegram from Sebastiani to Valdameri
25 October 1938
The DUCE will receive you at the Palazzo Venezia along with Gr. Uff. Alessandro Poss and the architects Terragni-Lingeri Thursday, November tenth, at 18 hours (6:30 pm). I would desire courtesy of an indication sent to Rome. Present this telegram to gain access to the Palace.
Personal Secretary
Sebastiani

Telegram from Valdameri to Sebastiani

27 October 1938

I thank you kindly for your interest and courteous communication. On Thursday, November Tenth, at 6:30 pm, I will arrive at the Palazzo Venezia along with Gr. Uff. Poss and Architects Lingeri and Terragni. We will be coming from the Hotel Ambasciatori.

With devoted cordiality,

Rino Valdameri

Notice of audience with Mussolini

10 November 1938

Lawyer Rino Valdameri is waiting in the anteroom to be received by Your Excellency. Rome 10/11/38, AXVII

Record of Mussolini's Personal Secretary *[probably Sebastiani]*

11 November 1938

His Excellency Alfieri this morning left 4 checks of 500,000 lire each (#005321/24), which is Poss's offer for Valdameri's *Danteum* project, hoping to have the Duce sign them, having forgotten to do so this morning.

Signed by Mussolini, "Consigned by me to the Prefect Luciano Bernabei, present"

11 November 1938 XVII

Letter from Massimo Bontempelli to Pietro Lingeri

4 February 1939

Venice 2/4/39 XVII

Dear Lingeri,

I received your letter yesterday with the *Relazione del Danteum*. But I have had the Album sent a while ago. Valdameri gave it to me on January 10; I brought it to Rome, where I was from the 22nd to the 25th of January; not having been able to see the Minister (he is perhaps in Pavia) I sent the Album to Marino Lazzari [Director General of the *Belle Arti* — the National Fine Arts Commission] telling him that for health reasons Valdameri had to go to Switzerland — having given me the responsibility of transporting it. Lazzari should have sent it by now to the Minister.

Therefore, you should send the Relazione immediately to Lazzari. I'll keep here all I've received, until you have given me word whether I should send it again or keep it for another occasion.
Many affectionate regards,
Your Massimo

Record of Mussolini's Personal Secretary
Extract from the record of Mr. Mileti
19 April 1939
To: Avv. Rino Valdameri
Albergo Ambasciatori
Through tomorrow, Thursday
Rome

His Excellency Sebastiani wished to entertain the following questions [only one pertains and is excerpted]: Present [to us] the necessity to be received by the Duce along with Gr. Uff. Poss, in relation to the "Danteum" foundation, when the Duce already indicated certain directives some time ago.
19/4/1939 XVII

Letter from Valdameri to Mussolini
20 April 1939
Rome, 20 April XVII

Duce, under your highest guidance our generation has the supreme pride in forging a new, iron destiny for our homeland.

I would be proud and happy to be able to dedicate my energies — still young — to the fervor of works that, through your vigor, the Camera dei Fasci e delle Corporationi [the Corporative Department of Government] is developing for the resurrection of our people.

In the Corporazione delle Sidurgia [Steel Corporation] I may place my contribution for much work in counseling that sector.

Duce, if, on your designation, I could have the honor of representing you in the Party — of which I have been a member since 1922 — in substitution for His Excellency Benini — my powers would know no fatigue or pause in serving you with unfailing enlightened faith and devotion.
Signed,
Rino Valdameri

Letter from Valdameri and Poss to Mussolini
2 May 1939
Milan 2 May 1939 XVII
To his Excellency Benito Mussolini
Head of State
Rome
Duce,

We have faithfully executed your orders. But in order that the "Danteum" rise on the Street of the Empire for [the Exposition of] 1942, it is necessary to place before you the work that we are accomplishing and that which develops.

We beg of you, therefore, Duce, to benevolently grant us the honor of an audience.
Rino Valdameri
Alessandro Poss

Letter from Valdameri to Colonel Nanni
31 May 1939
Most Kind Colonel,

It would be a great courtesy [to us] if you would add a copy of the two letters I have sent, as you counseled, to His Excellency for the Duce.

I have not yet heard a response. May I hope [for one]? With courageously recognizable devotion,
Rino Valdameri

Telegram from Sebastiani to Valdameri
5 June 1939
The Duce requests expressly to receive you at the Palazzo Venezia, along with Alessandro Poss, Thursday the eighth of this month at 1800 hours. I would request the courtesy of an indication sent to Rome. Present this telegram for access to the Palace.
Personal Secretary
Sebastiani

Telegram from Valdameri and Poss to Sebastiani

5 June 1939

Excellency Sebastiani,

We thank you for the communication concerning the possibility of an audience on Thursday the eighth. Meanwhile we wish you to confirm. We will communicate from our address at the Ambasciatori Hotel.

Avv. Valdameri

Comm. Poss.

Telegram from Valdameri to Sebastiani

6 June 1939

His Excellency Sebastiani, Personal Secretary to the Duce, Rome. Thank you for your communication. I am honored to assure you that Thursday the eighth of this month at 1800 hours I will arrive at the Palazzo Venezia with Alessandro Poss. I'll be at the Hotel Ambasciatori again. With grateful heart,

Rino Valdameri

Note from Ferri to Sebastiani

8 July 1939

[this records a telephone communication]

[He] asks His Excellency to let him know to when the audience that was granted and then suspended has been postponed.

Letter from Valdameri to Sebastiani

11 August 1939

To his Excellency Osvaldo Sebastiani

Personal Secretary to the Head of State

Excellency, In a telegram dated 5 June you courteously communicated to me that the Duce, addressing his expressed desire, would receive me with Gr. Uff. Alessandro Poss Thursday the eighth of June at the Palazzo Venezia.

By telephone that audience was put off.

Permit me to ask you to place your good offices [forward] so that the Duce might want to grant to Gr. Uff. Alessandro Poss (via Monteforte 50, Milan) and me the honor of an audience requested for 2 May to place before him the work that has been accomplished and that

which needs to be done from whence the "Danteum" can be erected on the Street of the Empire according to the orders of the Head of State. With special gratitude,
much devoted Rino Valdameri

Letter from Sebastiani to Valdameri

4 September 1939
[this was written four days after Hitler invaded Poland to begin WWII]
Avv. Rino Valdameri
Villa Valdameri
PORTOFINO

I would like to respond to your letter of 11 August in a more pleasant way. The actual moment does not, however, permit me to do so. In more favorable times you may be able to renew the request.

[End of the extant correspondence. Note: The abrupt change in the letters of Sebastiani's tone, from authoritarian to conciliatory and understanding, is perhaps an unconscious signal to the ensuing events of the World War.

Valdameri died of pneumonia in 1943. Terragni died of an embolism on 19 July 1943. (Some historians maintain that Terragni committed suicide, but I know of no hard evidence to support the claim.) Lingeri threw his fascist party pin out of a train window on 25 July 1943, the day Mussolini was deposed. He died in 1968 at the age of 70.]

Cover of the catalogue for the fascist revolution,
showing bust of Mussolini.

INDEX

Abstract forms 70, 72, 81, 136–37, 142–43, 144
Acropolis 54
Aizpurua 73n8
Albergo Posta Hotel (Terragni) 44
Alberti, Leone Battista 89, 139
Alfieri 157
Allegory 147–48, 149
Aquinega, de 73n8
Architectural adjective 139
Architecture
  importance of 138
  literature and 8–9, 11, 24, 42, 135–54
Architecture, Italian
  affect of Mussolini on 13–14, 15
  fascism and 13–14, 15, 18, 51, 53, 56, 147
  Piacentini criticism of 14–15
Argan, Giulio Carlo 13–14, 137
Autarchia (self-sufficiency) 16, 70

Baldessari, Luciano 76, 78
Bardi, Pietro Maria 147
Baroque Stair 54
Basilica of Constantine 51
Basilica of Maxentius 7, 24, 25, 51, 57, 79, 81, 85
Bauhaus complex 42
BBPR group (Benfi, Belgioiosi, Peressutti, Rogers) 53
Behrens, Peter 42
Bernabei, Luciano 157
Bernini, Giovanni Lorenzo 56
Bertoia, Il 86
Black, Max 148
Bonfanti, Ezio 7–8
Bontempelli, Massimo 7–8, 9, 22, 24, 135–36, 137, 139, 157
Brechtbuhl 73n8
Brera Academy 19, 70

Cantonal Library of Lugano (Terragni) 66
Carminati, Antonio 48, 73n20
Carrà, Carlo 9
Casa a Gradoni (Terragni) 66
Casa del Fascio at Como (Terragni) 4, 5, 7, 16, 18, 36n11, 42, 44, 48, 60, 73n20, 144, 149
Casa del Fascio at Lissone (Terragni) 44, 73n20
Casa del Fascio at Rome (Terragni) 63, 70
Casa del Floricoltore (Terragni) 44, 60, 63, 66, 70, 79
Casa Giuliani-Frigerio (Terragni) 60, 70, 72, 139
Casa Littorio. *See* Palazzo Littorio
Casa Toninello (Terragni) 48
Cattaneo, Cesare 70
Choisy drawing of a Roman vault 54, 56
Circle. *See* Geometric order
Cities: function of, in fascism 36n4
Classicism 8, 11, 44
Colosseum 78, 144
Columns 15, 16, 28–29, 36n7, 78, 86, 89, 91, 139, 143, 148–49
Content 42, 136–37, 138, 140, 151
Convivio (Dante) 85, 139, 149
Croce, Benedetto 21, 136–37, 137–38, 138–39, 143
Cylinder. *See* Columns; Geometric order

Dante Alighieri
  content and 140
  Convivio 85, 139, 145
  Croce's interpretation of 137–38
  De Monarchia 85, 139
  Epistle to Can Grande Della Scala 140–41, 142, 145
  fascism and 19, 20, 140, 146
  form and 140

164

meaning and 140, 142
Relazione sul Danteum and 135–54
structure and 140, 142
Valdameri's interest in 19
Vita Nuova 20
See also Danteum; *Divine Comedy*
Danteum
  as elaboration of absolute form 8–9
  as example of relationship between
  architecture and literature 8–9,
  11, 42, 135–54
  authorship of 24, 37n29, 37n30
  classicism and 11
  content of 137, 151
  correspondence about 21–22, 156–58,
  161–62
  design of 22, 25–35, 66, 70, 72,
  86, 89, 137, 138–39, 141–42, 144
  directorate for 20–21, 155–56
  Divine Comedy and 5, 8–9, 20,
  22, 25–35, 137, 138–39
  fascism and 19–22, 33, 91, 149
  form and 8–9, 140–41, 151
  fourfold exegisis and 145–49
  function of 20, 22, 155
  geometric order in 42, 78, 79, 81,
  142, 144–45
  influence of other Terragni work
  on 54, 66, 70
  influences of other people's work
  on 76, 81, 85
  Le Corbusier's view of 152
  metaphysical dimension of 5, 7
  Mussolini and 18, 19–22, 37n18, 151
  nationalism and 20, 32–33, 91
  problems of building 21–22, 24
  progression in 141
  Rocchi's view of 44
  Scheme A of 75, 76–77
  Statute 155–56
  structure of 5, 8–9, 142
  transcendence and 141–42
  Valdameri and 19–22, 155–58,

161–62
  See also Dante Alighieri;
  Divine Comedy;
  Epistle to Can Grande Della Scala;
  Relazione sul Danteum;
  Terragni, Giuseppe
De Monarchia (Dante) 85, 139
De Seta, Cesare 44
De Stijl movement 153n56
Distribuzione di Benzina
  Standardizzato (Terragni) 41
Divine Comedy 95–133
  as a memory book 137
  as part of Dante's experiences 8
  Danteum and 5, 8–9, 20, 22, 25–35,
  137, 138–39
  fascism and 19, 25
  form and 8–9, 143
  geometric organization of 78
  Relazione sul Danteum and
  95–133, 137–39
  structure and 138
  transcendence and 140–41
  See also Dante Alighieri; Danteum;
  Epistle to Can Grande Della Scala;
  Relazione sul Danteum

Eagle 151
Egypt 53, 54, 85
Eisenman, Peter 36n11
Epistle to Can Grande Della Scala
  (Dante) 140–41, 142, 145
Erba monument (Terragni) 44
Essence 142–44
Expression 136–37

Fascism
  Casa del Fascio as symbol of 18
  Dante and 19, 20, 140, 146
  Danteum and 19–22, 33, 91, 149
  Divine Comedy and 19, 25
  Italian architecture and 13–14, 15, 18,
  51, 53, 56, 147

patronage and 22, 157
See also Mussolini, Benito
Felice, Renzo di 37n26
Ferri 161
Figini, Luigi 19, 53, 70
Form 8–9, 136–37, 140–41, 143,
  149, 151
Forum (Trajan) 56
Fourfold exegesis 145–49
Frame architecture 89, 91
Freedberg, Sydney 86

Gentile, Giovanni 21
Geometric order 42, 72, 78, 79,
  81, 89, 91, 92n9, 136, 140, 141,
  142, 143–45, 153n56. *See also* Columns;
  Danteum: design of
Germany 51, 60, 63, 72.
  See also Hitler, Adolph
  Golden House of Nero (Rome) 76
  Golden section 72, 81, 140, 141, 144.
  See also Geometric order
Gropius 60, 63
Gruppo Sette 5, 56

History, Terragni's concept of 4, 5,
  53–54, 56–57, 70, 72, 76,
  85–86, 89, 136, 144, 147
Hitler, Adolph 15, 21, 162

International Style 13, 14, 16,
  75, 89, 91, 139
Intuition 136–37, 143

Karnak Temple 85

Latrobe, Benjamin 16
Lazzari, Marino 22, 24, 157–58

Lenkeith, Nancy 147
Le Corbusier
  aesthetic retreat and views of 16
  attitude about Danteum of 152

frame concept of 89
House for a College President 66, 70
Immeuble Type V-R 70
inability to categorize 91
influence on Terragni of 42, 48, 56,
  57, 63, 66, 70, 72, 76, 79, 81, 148
justification concept of 144
Liège Bata Pavillon 63, 70
Maison Citrohan 63
Maison Dom-ino 63
Maison Plainex 44
meaning and 143
Museum of the Square Spiral 66, 76
nationalism and 13
Nestlè Pavilion 63
Oeuvre Complète 1934–1938 70
rationalism and 36n2
Salvation Army Building (Paris) 57
speech (1933) by 11
Stadium for 100,000 Spectators 70
view of "happy towns" of 14
Villa Carthage 63
Villa Savoye 63
Villa Stein 63, 79, 81
Libera, Adalberto 18
Lictor's tower *(torre Littorio)*
  14, 51, 66, 73n20
Lingeri, Editta 37n18, 37n30
Lingeri, Piercarlo 37n18, 73n7
Lingeri, Pietro 19, 22, 24, 37n29,
  37n30, 70, 73n7, 139, 157, 162

Maison La Roche (Terragni) 66
Mambretti Tomb (Terragni) 76
Meaning 140, 142, 143, 145
Mendelsohn, Erich 42
Michelucci, Giovanni 51
Mies van der Rohe 63, 89, 143
Milan Apartment Houses (Terragni)
37n29
Milanese neoclassicism 4–5, 7
Mondrian, Piet 153n56

Monumentalists 42, 91
  See also Piacentini, Marcello
Motifs of Terragni 66, 70, 76, 85–86,
  91, 141, 142, 144
Mussolini, Benito
  affect of Italian architectural
  movement of 13–14, 15
  alliance with Hitler by 15
  architects' view of 14, 15
  concept of fascism as a glass house 18
  Danteum and 18, 19–22, 37n18, 151,
  156–58, 161-62
  influence of M. Sarfatti on 37n26
  Romanist view of 22
  See also Fascism; *Relazione sul Danteum*
Muzio, Giovanni 4, 5, 7, 8, 75

Nationalism 13, 14, 15, 18, 20,
  32–33, 91. *See also* Fascism
Nattini, Amos 19
Nizzoli, Marcello 48, 89
Novocumum Apartments at Como
  (Terragni) 42, 44
Nursing Home at Kassel 44

Officina per la Produzione del
  Gas (Terragni) 41, 42, 57, 60
Ojetti, Ugo 15, 21, 91, 139

Pagano, Giuseppe 4, 15, 16
Palace of Sargon in Persia 85
Palazzo dei Congressi (Terragni) 70
Palazzo Farnese 48
Palazzo Littorio (Terragni) 24, 48,
  51–57, 66, 70, 76, 81, 85
Palladio, Andrea 5
Parthenon 54, 89
Perls, Frederick 143
Peterson, Steven 143
Piacentini, Marcello 4, 14–15, 16, 18,
  36n5, 36n8, 44, 51, 91, 139
Pirandello, Luigi 138–39
Pirovano Tomb (Terragni) 73n7

Pollini, Gino 19, 53, 70
Poss, Count Alessandro 19, 21, 156,
  157, 158, 161
Progression 141
Radice, Mario 60, 70
Rationalism 8, 13, 15, 16, 18, 36n2,
  42, 53, 75, 89, 91
Raymond, Antonin 44
Rectangle. *See* Geometric order
Relazione sul Danteum
  (Report on the Danteum) 95–133
  compared to *Epistle to Can Grande
  Della Scala* 140–41, 142, 145
  contents of 24–35
  copy of, given to Mussolini 157–58
  Dante and 135–54
  Divine Comedy and 137–39
  geometric order and 78, 79, 92n9
  missing parts of 24
  nationalism in 18
  writing of 22, 24, 33, 35, 37n16
Ridolfi, Mario 18
Rocchi, Lorenzo 41, 44, 86
Roman theater 54, 56
Romano, Giulio 89
Rowe, Colin 89

Saint Abbondio, church of 36n14, 86
Saint Augustine 141
Saint Francis 20
Saint Paul 145
Saliva, Antonio 48
Salvisberg 73n8
Sangallo, Antonio the Younger 89
Sarfatti Monument (Terragni) 37n26, 66
Saubaudia (town) 36n4
Schoonmakers 153n56
Schroder House in Utrecht 44
Scuola Media competition (1934) 44
Sebastiani, Osvaldo 21–22,
  156–58, 161–62
Sequence 142–44
Sera, La 53

Serlio 85
Sironi, Mario 9, 22, 51, 151
Soviet Union: influence on
  Terragni of 60, 63, 72
Speer, Albert 14
Square. See Geometric order
Stalin, Joseph 15
Stampa, La 21
Stazione di Servizio e Benzina
  (Terragni) 70
Stazione di Servizio Standardizzato
  (Terragni) 63
Steel Manufacturing Corporation 21
Structure 5, 8–9, 138, 140, 142
Tafuri, Manfredo 4, 5, 7
Temple at Paestum 54, 56
Temple at Philae 53
Terragni, Giuseppe
  aesthetic experimentation of 60, 63
  architecture and its relationship
  to literature for 8–9, 11, 24,
  42, 135–54
  Catholicism of 18, 35, 36n14, 140
  classicism and 8, 11, 44
  content in work of 42, 136–37, 138
  death of 15
  design theory of 148
  form in the work of 136–37
  frame view of 89, 91
  historical concept of 4, 5, 53–54,
  56–57, 70, 72, 76, 85–86, 89,
  136, 144, 147
  identification with Dante of 139–54
  materials used by 16
  metaphysical aspects of 4–5, 7–8,
  9, 11, 36n14, 143
  military service of 86
  motifs of 66, 70, 76, 85–86, 91,
  141, 142, 144
  structure and 9, 142
  urbanism and 5
  See also Danteum; Epistle to Can
  Grande Della Scala; Geometric

order; Relazione sul Danteum;
  Terragni, Giuseppe, criticisms of;
  Terragni, Giuseppe, influences on;
  Terragni, Giuseppe, works of
Terragni, Giuseppe, criticisms of:
  by Argan 13–14, 137
  by de Seta 44
  by Eisenman 36n11
  by Pagano 4
  by Rocchi 41, 44
  by Tafuri 4, 7
  by Zevi 36n11
Terragni, Giuseppe, influences on:
  of abstract forms 70, 72, 81, 136–37
  of Baldessari 76, 78
  of Bertoia 86
  of Bontempelli 7–8, 9, 22, 24, 135–36
  contemporary 70
  of Croce 136–37, 137–38
  Egyptian 53, 54, 85
  German/Soviet 60, 63, 72
  of Gropius 42, 60, 63
  of history 4, 5, 53–54, 56–57, 70,
  72, 76, 85–86, 89, 136, 144, 147
  of Le Corbusier 42, 48, 56, 57, 63,
  66, 70, 72, 76, 79, 81, 148
  of Milanese neoclassicist group 4–5, 7
  of Radice 60, 70
  See also Dante Alighieri;
  Geometric order; Relazione sul Danteum;
  Terragni, Giuseppe; Terragni, Giuseppe,
  criticisms of; Terragni,
  Giuseppe, works of
Terragni, Giuseppe, works of
  Albergo Posta Hotel 44
  Brera Academy building 19, 70
  Cantonal Library of Lugano 66
  Casa a Gradoni 66
  Casa del Fascio (Como) 4, 5, 7, 16,
  18, 36n11, 42, 44, 48, 60,
  73n20, 144, 149
  Casa del Fascio (Lissone) 44, 73n20
  Casa del Fascio (Rome) 63, 70

Casa del Floricoltore (Rebbio) 44, 60, 63, 70, 79
Casa Giuliani-Frigerio 60, 70, 72, 139
Casa Toninello (Milan) 48
Distribuzione di Benzina Standardizzato 41
Erba monument 44
Maison La Roche 66
Mambretti Tomb 76
Milan Apartment Houses 37n29
Novocumum Apartments (Como) 42, 44
Officina per la Produzione del Gas 41, 42, 57, 60
Palazzo dei Congressi 70
Palazzo Littorio 24, 48, 51–57, 66, 70, 76, 81, 85
Pirovano Tomb 73n7
Sarfatti Monument 37n26, 66
Scuola Media competition 44
Stazione di Servizio e Benzina 70
Stazione di Servizio Standardizzato 63
Tomba Pirovano 44
Tomba Stecchini 44
Villa Bianca 66
Villa sul Lago 63, 66
Tomba Pirovano (Terragni) 44

Tomba Stecchini (Terragni) 44
Torre dei Conti 24
Torre Littorio (Lictor's tower) 14, 51, 66, 73n20
Transcendence 140–41
Tyrins, complex at 53

Valdameri, Rino 19–22, 37n16, 155–58, 161–62
Van Doesburg, Theo 153n56
Vesna School at Brno 44
Vietti 48, 73n9
Vignola, Giacomo da 89
Villa Bianca 66
Villa sul Lago (Terragni) 63, 66
Virgil 41, 78
Vita Nuova (Dante) 20

Wolin, Judith 154n60

Yates, Frances 137

Zevi, Bruno 36n5, 36n8, 36n11
Zuccoli, Luigi 36n14, 37n18, 37n30, 148

169